"Valorie Kondos Field's scope goes well beyond gymnastics … Miss Val is the life coach we all need in our corner, be it in the boardroom or in the arena. I encourage all CEOs who want to tap into their fullest potential to become a student of Coach Val."

—Mary Callahan Erdoes, CEO,
J.P. Morgan Asset & Wealth Management

"Miss Val's not-as-you-would-expect approach to coaching has positioned her to ink 7 NCAA Championships. Her success has inspired many who have witnessed her gifts and genius as a coach, mentor, and healer."

—William D. Parham, PhD, ABPP, director, Mental Health and Wellness Program for NBA Players Association

"Miss Val is a force of nature. Her journey to the top is a riveting story. Her demand for personal excellence and her ability to create belief in her student athletes provide for a great read and success model for all."

—Sue Enquist, founder of ONE Softball, former UCLA head softball coach and 11-time National Champion

"After years of observation I can say with unbridled respect and full-throttled enthusiasm, 'It is Miss Val's turn!' She truly is one of the brightest beacons of light in the gymnastics world!"

—Kathy Johnson Clarke, sports commentator and 1984 Olympic medalist

LIFE IS SHORT, DON'T WAIT *to Dance*

Advice and Inspiration from the UCLA Athletics Hall of Fame Coach of 7 NCAA Championship Teams

VALORIE KONDOS FIELD

with Steve Cooper

CENTER STREET

New York   Nashville

Center Street
Hachette Book Group
1290 Avenue of the Americas, New York, NY 10104
centerstreet.com
twitter.com/centerstreet

First published in hardcover and ebook in October 2018
First Trade Paperback Edition: October 2019

Center Street is a division of Hachette Book Group, Inc. The Center Street name and logo are trademarks of Hachette Book Group, Inc.

The publisher is not responsible for websites (or their content) that are not owned by the publisher.

The Hachette Speakers Bureau provides a wide range of authors for speaking events. To find out more, go to www.HachetteSpeakersBureau.com or call (866) 376- 6591.

Library of Congress Cataloging-in-Publication Data has been applied for.

ISBNs: 978-1-5460-7712-1 (trade paperback), 978-1-5460-7713-8 (ebook)

This book is dedicated to my mom.
You were with us for such a short time but
your example of how to love unconditionally
was a gift to all who knew you.

Contents

A Note from Nan Wooden

A few years back me, Valorie, and five of our close girlfriends took a trip to Vegas. I was in my late 70s and thought it would be fun to visit Australia's Thunder from Down Under (the male revue show). Without getting too detailed, I can admit it was a memorable night, one in which I found myself up onstage with the lovely accented and very handsome Aussie host. While Valorie denies it, I believe she was behind my appearance onstage.

For people who know Valorie, this story isn't shocking. She has a way of making those around her feel safe to trust, and inspired to get creative and to be adventurous. Valorie's journey from professional ballerina to one of the most successful college gymnastics coaches of all time is only possible because of how she makes people feel. They have to trust her. The championships her teams have won have come from her focusing more on her student-athletes' success in life than anything else.

I don't think it's a coincidence that Olympians from around the world come to her program. These are athletes who have already achieved the highest level of success in their athletic careers, but they gravitate toward Valorie because they know she is going to make them better people.

I felt very close to Valorie from the beginning of our friendship. Our relationship has continued to grow closer with each passing year. She refers to herself as my "curly haired daughter," which is a welcome addition to my existing three daughters. We also share a special bond, as we are both breast cancer survivors.

When people hear about the antics Valorie and I get up to, they are often surprised at how close she became to my dad, legendary basketball coach John Wooden. He had been retired for decades before the two ever met. The thing is, Valorie and I are very much alike in spirit—which also makes us similar in nature to that of my mother, Nellie.

Daddy was a quiet, buttoned-down gentleman. His full name was John Roberts and so my grandparents called him John Bob. One of my favorite stories is when my mom's folks said to her while they were dating, "Nellie, we really like John Bob, but we're really just afraid he's not going to amount to anything." Of course, he went on to become the greatest college basketball coach in history.

This is the first point of similarity between Valorie and my dad. People underestimated what they were capable of because they didn't understand their inner drive for excellence. My dad and Valorie were very different, but they shared the same values. My dad cared deeply for those around him and wanted them to succeed; Valorie is the same way.

Early in his career my mom wanted Daddy to succeed and was the free spirit that I believe helped push him to greatness. She encouraged him to take a public speaking class because he was so shy. He trusted her, took the class, and gained more confidence because of it.

My dad was attracted to my mom's loving strength and I believe he saw that in Valorie from the moment they connected. In kind, Valorie married Bobby Field, a former UCLA football coach, who has the same quiet, calm demeanor as my dad that provides the balance in their relationship.

In truth, it was Bobby who knew my father before Valorie did. However, just as my mother pushed Daddy to stand up and speak, it was Valorie who pushed Bobby to pick up the phone and invite my dad over for their first dinner together.

A lot of people in this world will have dreams, but there's a lot of work that goes on in the background to make those dreams come true. Daddy was meticulous in his preparation. Valorie is meticulous in the life lessons she teaches her young student-athletes through gymnastics. Neither of them was successful by accident. My dad was intentional with what he wanted and went after it; Valorie has done the same thing.

Their relationship happened because Valorie did the work. Valorie was the one who asked Bobby to set up the dinner. Valorie was the one who invited Daddy to attend the women's gymnastics meets. Their relationship wasn't luck or coincidence, their relationship happened because Valorie made it happen and they bonded because the chemistry was right.

Before Valorie invited him, Daddy had never attended a UCLA women's gymnastics meet. Once he saw how Valorie treated her athletes he was hooked. My dad cared for his players, but watching the outward affection shown by Valorie and the reciprocation by her girls was a new and exciting experience for him.

My dad won more NCAA basketball championships than any coach in history, but his definition of success doesn't include the word "winning." Valorie comes from a background of dance where there's no such thing as winning, only doing your best to have a successful performance. The two spoke the same coaching language.

Daddy's impact on this world has reached far beyond his 10 national championships in 12 years. His Pyramid of Success has become a favorite teaching tool of many CEOs. I believe Valorie is in the process of delivering that same influence in her own unique way.

Prologue

February 19, 2017

I turned on the television to watch *60 Minutes* and braced myself. I knew that what I was about to hear was going to be extremely disturbing. Jessica Howard, Jeanette Antolin, and Jamie Dantzscher, former members of US women's gymnastics national teams, were going to describe in detail the sexual abuse they had suffered from the USA Gymnastics' (USAG) national team doctor, Larry Nassar. They were to become the highest-profile voices among the more than 60 women who, by then, had already filed complaints against Nassar.

So what was it, in particular, that distressed me about the *60 Minutes* piece I was about to watch? It was that two of the women, Jeanette and Jamie, had been members of the UCLA gymnastics team from 2000 to 2004 and I had been their head coach. During the years Jeanette and Jamie were in our program, I could see that each of them was holding in some deep emotional pain, but I had no idea what they had gone through. Both acted out at times and definitely had trust issues. Even though I had no idea of the abuse they had suffered, I was the one who needed to earn their trust and empower them to trust their own voices moving forward.

I listened as Jamie told Jon LaPook, the *60 Minutes* interviewer, that she was initially sent to see Nassar in 1995, when, as a member of the US junior national team, she started having bad lower back pain. She described the inappropriate touching that occurred during her very first "procedure" with the team doctor. She was just 13 years old. The "procedures" continued for the next five years as Jamie worked her way on to the 2000 bronze medal Olympic team.

Jeanette also described the sexual assault she suffered from Nassar at the now infamous Karolyi Ranch, which was then the USA Gymnastics National Team Training Center on the property of legendary gymnastics coaches Martha and Bela Karolyi in Texas. When asked why she didn't tell anyone her concerns about the treatments, she replied, "It was treatment. You don't complain about treatment."

The women, who are now in their 30s, made it clear in the interview that no one on the US national team complained about anything. Jamie talked about the verbal abuse she and her fellow gymnasts routinely received at the ranch. She described how the Karolyis' method of teaching was to consistently demean, intimidate, and insult the athletes, constantly reminding them they weren't good enough. There was enormous pressure to be perfect.

These women were describing an established culture of coaching through intimidation that has been widely accepted in sport for decades. The goal was to win at any cost. Coaches and others in positions of authority, like Nassar, were protected instead of the athletes.

As members of the USAG program, the athletes had been coached to be the greatest gymnasts in the world. When they won gold they were lauded as champions by the national training staff and USAG. When they faltered and didn't win gold, but "merely" the silver or bronze—or didn't medal—they were publicly humiliated and chastised by those same people. This small handful of individuals didn't speak for the entire gymnastics community, but they did yield the most power, in every way, over our athletes.

Those who grew up in the US gymnastics system were taught to ignore their inner voices. Jeanette once told me it wasn't that their opinions didn't matter, it was that they were taught to not have opinions. These gymnasts were treated like interchangeable cogs in a machine. The most egregious case I experienced was with former national team member Mattie Larson. After her floor performance at the 2010 world championships when she failed to complete her final tumbling pass successfully, Mattie was immediately shunned by her coaches and Martha. She told me that she would pinch herself to see if she was alive because she literally felt invisible. Three years later, during her sophomore year at UCLA, Mattie broke. Just outside our gym door she began crying and hysterically screaming, "Miss Val, please don't make me go in that gym. I just can't anymore." Everything she had experienced previously was now surfacing in our gym. Imagine the abuse and mental trauma it took for her to reach that point.

In 2012 at the London Olympics, I asked the then president of USAG, Steve Penny, why we as a country allowed Martha Karolyi to treat our athletes with such verbal and emotional abuse. The entirety of his reply was, "She wins."

I countered with, "At what cost?"

That question was met with dismissive silence.

Many of us club and college coaches have been trying to pick up the pieces of the broken system for decades. My goal has always been to help all athletes unearth, embrace, and develop the strength that is already inside them, no matter how deeply buried or how long suppressed.

As of this writing, more than 300 women have come forward with allegations against Larry Nassar. Many top gymnasts have also complained or have alleged wrongdoing against USAG, the US Olympic Committee (USOC), and the FBI. Nassar has been sentenced to over 200 years in prison. The presidents of USAG and of the USOC have resigned, as has the entire USAG board of directors. The investigation into abuse within the sport remains ongoing and has expanded to all sports under the USOC purview.

In June of 2018, Rhonda Faehn, who has gone from Olympic gymnast to UCLA gymnast to collegiate coach and full circle back into the elite program as senior vice president of USAG, was questioned during a US Senate subcommittee hearing as part of the investigation. Rhonda was fired from her position just weeks before appearing, and to date USAG hasn't given an explanation. During her opening statement to the senators, Rhonda said, "After my years on the national team, I earned a gymnastics scholarship to UCLA. It was there, under the guidance of coach Valorie Kondos Field, I began to realize I wanted to make a positive impact on the lives of athletes."

While the circumstances for hearing that statement were painful, I am touched to know that it was in our program at UCLA that Rhonda had that realization.

When Jamie and Jeanette competed as UCLA Bruins, they played a major role in our NCAA championship wins in 2001, 2003, and 2004.

In 2002, in addition to the team championship, Jamie won three additional titles: for all-around athlete, floor exercise, and vault. During her four years at UCLA, Jamie achieved 28 perfect 10s, setting a school record yet to be broken. In recognition of her accomplishments, in 2016, Jamie was inducted into the UCLA Athletics Hall of Fame.

As for Jeanette, she began training at the age of three. At age 14, in 1995, she earned a spot on the US national team and, during the next five years, was a vital member of our US national team, earning numerous medals.

Jeanette then became a valuable member of the UCLA Bruins women's gymnastics team and fully blossomed in 2004 when she became the Pac-10 Gymnast of the Year and was also named the *Sports Illustrated on Campus* National Gymnast of the Year. It was the year she performed an *insane* seven perfect 10s in a row on vault! She also achieved a UCLA record 10 perfect 10s for the season.

Nothing, however, has made me prouder of these two women than when I witnessed their courage in telling their stories, lending their strong voices to those of all the other brave athletes who have spoken out. At Nassar's sentencing hearing in January 2018,

Jeanette, Jamie, and Mattie were among the 156 women who gave impact statements. Each of the women who came forward enumerated unapologetic facts about the abuse they suffered. Each of them spoke with clarity and confidence. And while quite a few got emotional and angry, none of them lost their composure and poise. That inner strength, that commitment to purpose, that ability to look their abuser in the eye and not waiver or be intimidated is what I believe nearly all of them learned through the discipline of years of involvement in gymnastics. And their courageously unflinching impact statements made it clear: Time's Up.

I am thankful that these brave women have found their voices and won't stop speaking out until change happens. This is *their* sport. It is a thrilling and beautiful sport and it will be forever changed for the better, thanks to them. I am also delighted to share with you that after Mattie Larson broke and dropped out of school she came full circle, finished her degree, and attended a gymnastics meet where we honored her and other sexual abuse victims.

Know that this book isn't about gymnastics, and the advice I share isn't just for gymnasts, athletes, or coaches. From classrooms to boardrooms and everywhere in between, we're often discouraged to speak our minds and tell our truths. This book isn't about litigating abuses, and I am not here to play judge and jury. My goal is to empower you to find your voice. Identify obstacles, silence the noise, listen to your inner dialogue, and determine your truth.

Make life your own great adventure. When you think about

your favorite adventure stories you'll realize there is no failure, just obstacles to overcome that then become the most exciting part of the story. Be intentional with your thoughts and your actions and embrace the power that comes with taking responsibility for them. If your voice is ignored, stay on course. You don't need to feel intimidated or bullied or waiver from what you know to be true.

I teach our student-athletes that the choices they make dictate the life they lead. So, to understand the choices I've made (or haven't made) let me share a little of my history....

LIFE IS SHORT, DON'T WAIT to *Dance*

Chapter One

From Ballerina to Coach

"Making a big life change is scary. But what's even scarier... Regret."

—ZIG ZIGLAR

I was 22 years old when I picked up the phone and made the call. It was a choice that changed my life. It was 1982 and I was a professional ballet dancer preparing for my debut season with the Washington Ballet when I heard UCLA needed a dance coach and choreographer for their gymnastics team. I flew to Los Angeles to meet with the head coach, Jerry Tomlinson, and was offered the job. During the interview I was told they couldn't offer me a salary, but they could provide a full scholarship to attend UCLA. Attending UCLA had always been my dream. Throughout high school, while I was dancing and taking piano lessons, I dreamed of going to UCLA and being a tall, tan, blond volleyball player. The only part of that equation I could ever achieve was the tan part—thanks to my Greek heritage. When I was offered a full scholarship at UCLA it was the closest I could imagine to being a student-athlete. (I wasn't on the volleyball team and I hadn't grown an extra foot or dyed my hair blond, but still, I was ecstatic.) I flew back to DC, packed up my belongings, retired from dancing, and moved to Los Angeles to join the prestigious coaching staff of the UCLA gymnastics team.

Today, I am the UCLA women's gymnastics head coach. In 1997 I led the program to its first national championship—a feat we've achieved a total of seven times. I've been honored as the NCAA Coach of the Year four times; in 2010 I was inducted into the UCLA Athletic Hall of Fame; and in 2016 I was named the Pac-12 Coach of the Century.

How did all of that happen? I have never done gymnastics! In fact, I have never participated in competitive sports! I have never flipped. I have never launched my body off a vault or performed on that harrowing four-inch balance beam. And yet, I have been the head coach of one of the most successful sports programs in the country for over a quarter century.

When I look back at my history, it's very clear that choice is where it all begins. Choice is the opportunity to *choreograph my life*. Most people hear "choreography" and they immediately think dance. I describe choreography as any *intentional movement*. Think about it…choreography is movement that you are either instructed to do or choose to do on your own. Either way it's intentional. I've come to understand that each choice will have numerous repercussions. It can be as daunting and paralyzing as it is exciting and liberating. Life is about choice, and the choices I make will dictate the life I lead.

In writing this book, I realized that every thing positive in my life has come from something I intentionally chose to do. Intentional choice comes from being able to honor your own voice. I've always been able to do this because of the people in my life who encouraged me to have an opinion, have a voice, and to own my actions. It started with my parents, Rosie and Gregory Kondos. As a child, art history books were strewn about my home because my father is an accomplished artist whose work is in the New York National Academy of Design. Visiting museums and attending art show openings were part of our normal life. It wasn't just the great works I was exposed to, I was also privileged to have the experience of being around extremely expressive people. One of my favorite people who frequented art openings was the Purple Lady, who dressed in head-to-toe purple at every event. I loved it! The art world was where I first became aware of the joy that comes from observing without judging. You can simply observe a work of art in so many different ways without labeling it as "good" or "bad." The artists I know embrace individuality as a badge of honor. Their uniqueness is at the heart of their craft. Years later, as a coach, perhaps this is partially why it was just second nature for me to nurture the individuality and uniqueness of each of our athletes.

Growing up, it was my mom, in particular, who did not pass judgments and who never put pressure on me or my brother, Steve, to be "the best." Some of my friends' parents did pressure them to excel, and I realized, even then, how much more joy I had because my mom just let us be. It was such a liberating feeling not to have to achieve a standard set by my parents. I could just savor life's experiences.

My mom also taught me that making a mistake was simply a way to learn something. I remember one night at the dinner table we were in the middle of a discussion when I spilled a glass of milk that blanketed the entire table. My mom didn't even flinch, she just kept on with our conversation while she retrieved a towel to mop up the mess. I laugh now because that was a living example of the proverb *Don't cry over spilled milk*. Because of her, I have always understood that learning and growing are what life is all about; consequently I did not grow up with a "fear of failure." I honestly do not acknowledge failure as something to be ashamed of. I believe it is just another "F-word" some mean-spirited person assigned a meaning to in an effort to make others feel bad. How can something be a failure if you've actually learned something from the experience? Failure provides feedback on how you can do something better. I continue to use the valuable life lessons they taught me and share those lessons with our athletes in and out of the gym.

Whenever we lose a championship meet, I always reflect on it and figure out what I can do better or differently the next time around. I discuss it with our staff and we formulate a plan to have better results at the next competition. I love the challenge of figuring out how to do better.

Whenever we win, as we did most recently in 2018, I celebrate with the team for a job well done, but, to be honest, I don't learn nearly as much. Of course, the winning part is really fun.

Perhaps for many of you, the idea of life being about choice is not new. In fact, it is found in many different spiritual teachings. I first contemplated this philosophy when I heard these words from John Wooden, the legendary UCLA men's basketball coach and my greatest mentor: "There is a choice you have to make in everything you do. So keep in mind that in the end, the choice you make, makes you."

Though he passed away in 2010, Coach Wooden continues to be an inspiration and powerful influence on my life. I think about him often and especially every time I enter our training gym, which is in the John Wooden Center. The very title of this book is in homage to him.

Coach Wooden lived an impeccable life, and yet in his later years, whenever he was asked if he had any regrets he would always say, "My wife, Nellie, loved to dance, and yet I never danced with her because I was shy and did not think I was a good dancer." Looking back, he realized that he should have made a different choice because it would have made Nellie—and thus, him—happy. No one would have cared if he were a good dancer or not. Anyone watching would have seen a couple who had met in high school and remained very much in love throughout their 52-year marriage. I heard him solemnly mention many times, "My biggest regret is that I didn't dance with my wife."

I have learned throughout various stages of my life, as you will read, to embrace the sentiment of the book title: think about and figure out what you want to do and then choose to do it. Live your life with no regrets...and don't wait, because life *is* short.

In a way, I also feel as if I had my own dance with Coach Wooden. He moved me to live a life I never would have dreamed of. He gave me permission to embrace my uniqueness and unapologetically share that with others. As you will see, very little about my life choices and me can be called traditional.

So, in keeping with that, neither is this book! What I am about to share is a combination of memoir, motivational messaging (I hope!), insights into the world of gymnastics, advice, and more. It is not my entire story and doesn't include all the wonderful, amazing individuals I have met along my journey, but, what is here supports my truth about finding your voice and embracing your choice. As you read, I hope you will see that it is possible to be successful even if you don't (and more likely because you don't) subscribe to the "normal" way of doing things. Imagine how boring our world would be if we were all the same. The only reason innovation exists in the first place is because someone dared to think outside the norm.

I have found life is much more fun when I stop waiting to see what it hands me and instead take charge without a concern about what's deemed normal. I invite you to be intentional with your choices and to choreograph your life one choice at a time.

Chapter Two

Dancing Through Life

"He has achieved success who has lived well, laughed often, and loved much."

—Bessie Anderson Stanley

When I was young my family would take frequent trips to Greece to visit our relatives. My mother's father and my father's mother were both from the same place in Greece, a small underdeveloped village called Amos that is right outside of Kalamata (where those amazing Greek olives are from). These trips had a tremendous impact on me.

Each visit was like traveling back in time. The floors in my grandfather's home in Amos were not finished; they were dirt. There was a bathtub in the kitchen, but it really wasn't used for baths as much as it was used for washing dishes and clothes. The toilet was in an outhouse, and you needed to make sure to take "the stick" with you so you could fight off the obnoxious rooster who seemed determined to prevent anyone from entering the structure.

Each morning I would help my grandfather tie the three goats and two sheep to the saddle of Maria the donkey. Then we would walk them all a half mile to the pasture where they'd spend the day doing whatever goats and sheep do all day. We'd go back home and I'd help wash the clothes in the bathtub, make the supper, and play with the neighboring kids.

The first time we went to Amos I was four years old. My dad was teaching art in Piraeus right outside of Athens. I remember I didn't want to stay in the city. Why would any kid want to stay in a city when she could live in the enchanted fairytale world of a *village*?! So my parents and brother stayed in Piraeus during the week and I stayed in Amos. I didn't know any Greek, but that didn't bother me. I had no problem asking my grandparents and young friends how to say things. I can still vividly remember, for instance, pointing to the rope that we were using to tie the goats to the donkey's saddle and asking my Papou (grandfather) how to say "rope" in Greek. It's *skoiní*.

It was during my second trip to Amos, when I was seven, that I understood something that has stayed with me ever since. My family in Greece didn't know that they were poor. They had a roof over their heads, they had food, they had purpose in their daily lives, they had friends and family, they broke out in song and dance whenever the spirit moved them, they knew God, they knew love. They wanted for nothing and were happy. They shockingly didn't know they were poor. Really poor. They didn't know, didn't care, and were a heck of a lot happier than a lot of people I knew back in the States. At that moment, I realized I didn't need loads of money in order for my life to be rich.

I have often thought about my days in Amos. The memories fill me with joy and my experiences there are a wonderful reminder of how abundant life can be when you appreciate what you have and live life to the fullest. I learned very young not to spend time comparing what I don't have to what someone else does have. I learned that it's all about your own perceptions and also about making what you *do have* work for you the best that you can. I learned, too, that there are so many different ways to live your life, that there is not one ideal way to be or one prescription for happiness that will work for everyone. We each get to choose that for ourselves.

Not only did I arrive at these thoughts when I was seven, I also had the opportunity to have them guide me through my experiences with dance classes. I started ballet at seven because I had scoliosis. The upper part of my spine was curved, and the doctors thought that ballet would be good for my back. I quickly learned I wasn't born to be a ballet dancer. My physical form and execution of technical skills did not conform to those of a classical ballerina and the art of ballet. I did not look like other dancers. I did not move with the technical precision of other dancers. But that didn't stop me, even though I would be told numerous times by different ballet directors, "Your head is too big, your neck is too short, your feet are too small, you have no turnout or flexibility." Invariably, they would add, "But you can *dance*."

I credit this to my Greek heritage and to my mother. The Greeks literally dance through life. Young and old (and very old), they are known for beautiful spontaneous movements whenever the spirit moves them, whether or not there is music. To this day I vividly remember my grandparents in Greece dancing in the kitchen before dinner, at every social function we attended, and almost always after dinner as we sat out on the back porch.

When I was 12, I had my first professional dance gig. It was with the Sacramento Ballet, and I was in the corps de ballet for the *Nutcracker*. I recall getting paid $200 for the entire season, which probably came out to about $10 a performance. The amount didn't matter. I remember thinking, "Wow, they think I'm good enough to pay me to dance!"

Dance continued to be my passion and I continued my training. Then, when I was 16 years old I decided to look for a summer job. Ever since I watched Olga Korbut in the 1972 Olympic Games I was fascinated with gymnastics, even though I had never taken a gymnastic class. So I called a local gymnastics club to see if they needed a dance coach for their gymnasts. While speaking with the head coach, Jim Stephenson, I mentioned that I played the piano. Jim told me that they didn't have money for a dance coach but were in desperate need of a pianist. This was at a time when the rules stated that only one instrument could be used for floor exercise music. The piano was the most commonly used instrument for that purpose, though every once in a while someone did use drums or a guitar instead.

So it was in 1976 that I landed my first non-dance job and my first job having to do with gymnastics. It was at the AgileLites School of Gymnastics. To this day I can't believe how fortunate I was to be taught the basics of gymnastics by Jim Stephenson. Along with being a great gymnastics coach, Jim was also a brilliant artist and sculptor. He educated me on each of the four events—vault, bars, beam, and floor—from an artist's perspective rather than strictly from an athletic playbook. He spoke my language when he explained gymnastics as performance art, basically taking everything I knew as a classical ballet dancer and adding the new dimensions (for me) of flipping and twisting.

It didn't take long before I was a pianist who offered my brash and unsolicited opinions on floor routines—a shock to no one who has ever met me. "Get your head up," I'd say with conviction. "Point your feet," or "Straighten your legs!" I'd call out to the gymnasts during their routines.

It was remarkable. Here I was, a teenager who had never done gymnastics, telling other teenagers what to do in their own sport. What was really remarkable was that they accepted my critiques and actually implemented them. I simply said them with enough conviction and chutzpah that people actually listened.

It wasn't long before I told Jim he should reconsider hiring me as a dance coach. Jim said, "Fine, but I need to know you can dance." I replied with my own "fine," laced up my pointe shoes, walked out onto the floor, and proceeded to perform a 5-minute ballet.

Shortly thereafter, I choreographed my first floor routine. It was for the oldest member of the team, Syd Jones, who was 17. She was wonderful—I was not. She was an accomplished gymnast—I had no idea what I was doing. And yet, I had no trepidation or hesitation... I just did my best.

Looking back, the routine was all wrong. Much of what I was asking her to do throughout the routine was extremely difficult *and* didn't satisfy the requirements in the gymnastics code of points, which made it totally useless in scoring. And yet, Syd tried everything I asked of her, and the routine eventually turned out nicely, even fulfilling the code of points. Syd had every reason to balk at what I was asking her to do, but she didn't. That says a lot about her character, confidence, and ability to live life outside her comfort zone.

The following year, I graduated from high school and considered going to college while continuing to dance. My dad sat me down and said, "Honey, your mom and I believe in the importance of higher education, but as an artist I know if you want to dance you need to give it your all. You can always go back to school, but you can't always dance. So if you still love it, you need to go and pursue your dreams as a dancer."

That was such an incredible gift! My parents gave me the support to pursue my dream of dancing without any guilt about putting off college. My parents encouraged my choice and made it safe for me to listen to my heart and my voice.

I went off to dance in New York and Washington, DC. In the spring of 1982 I had been taking classes at the Washington Ballet for a few months, when they held their auditions. I decided to sit them out. I was more than accustomed by now to hearing all the negative physical critiques because, let's face it, my head was *still* too big and my neck and feet were *still* too short. As for my turnout and flexibility, objectively, they had improved only slightly.

After the auditions, I was walking down the hall of the ballet studio when the ballet director stopped me and asked me why I hadn't auditioned. I told him I could simply see that every female dancer who had auditioned was the epitome of the lithe, uber-flexible ballerina with long legs, a beautiful long neck, and a small head. I wasn't having a pity party, I assured him, but I knew I more closely resembled a stout Greek folk dancer (case in point: in "Peter and the Wolf," I played the Wolf!). When I finished, the ballet director said, "Ah yes, but you can dance!" And with that, he offered me a position with the company, which I quickly and happily accepted.

However, I actually didn't get through even one season with the company. Shortly before we were due to start rehearsals, I heard that UCLA needed a dance coach and choreographer for their women's gymnastics team. I happened to be home and visiting the AgileLites gym when Trina Tinti, a beautiful elite gymnast and future UCLA Bruin, mentioned the UCLA opportunity to me.

While dancing was—and will always be—my deepest passion, UCLA was my dream. I always knew it was one of the top academic and athletic universities in the world, so when I had the opportunity to pursue that ambition I jumped at the chance.

Chapter Three

Enter Miss Val

"What's in a name?"

—WILLIAM SHAKESPEARE

I joined UCLA in the fall of 1982 as assistant coach and choreographer for the Bruins women's gymnastics team. After growing up and spending the majority of my life in a ballet studio, I relished and embraced being in the UCLA gym, filled with the haze of chalk dust. They also asked me to coach balance beam. I had no idea what the heck I was doing, so consequently I really didn't do much except marvel at what the human body could do. The gymnasts flipped and twisted and contorted their bodies with perfection. What shocked me the most was that their skill wasn't an aberration—the gymnasts did this every...single...day, multiple times per day.

It was a thrill to be involved with the amazing UCLA women's program, which trained alongside the illustrious men's gymnastics team. I remember teaching our athletes a ballet class, early on, when Lisa Taylor, one of the gymnasts, asked me in a smart-alecky tone, "Are we supposed to call you Miss Val?" In the dance world you call your teacher "Miss" instead of "Coach." I thought it was a fine idea. I replied, "Yeah, sure, call me Miss Val." And, since that day most people in the gymnastics world and others who know me professionally call me Miss Val. I think (I hope!) they do it because it has a nice ring to it. The cool kids shorten it to "Miss V" or "VKF." I'm fine with any of those; as long as no one calls me "Ma'am."

From 1982 to 1996 the women's team trained with the men's team. In the early 80's the men's team included some of the best gymnasts in the world. Peter Vidmar, Tim Daggett, and Mitch Gaylord, three of the "greatest of all time," would become part of the 1984 men's gymnastics team—the only gold medal–winning team in US men's gymnastics history! I got to watch these athletes train every day. In fact, Peter humbly asked me if I would clean up his floor routine and give him more polish and style. And as an added bonus, Mitch and I had a history class together. I felt like the coolest girl on campus because I got to ride on the back of Mitch's motorcycle every Tuesday and Thursday from class to the gym.

I settled in quickly to my classes and to being the balance beam coach and floor exercise choreographer for the women's team. In 1987 I graduated with a degree in history and was looking into becoming a journalist while still choreographing for UCLA and other university and club gymnastics programs. Three years later, I did not think much of being called into a meeting with our associate athletic director, Dr. Judith Holland. Imagine my surprise when she offered me the job of head coach of the team!

The UCLA women's gymnastics team was a powerhouse program; it often had the most talented gymnasts in the nation, but the team had never won an NCAA championship. We were runners-up twice in the 1980s. In 1989 we finished second to Georgia by 0.05 points counting two falls (that's counting a full point 1.0 in falls). To win a championship everything has to come together: great coaching, healthy athletes, good team chemistry, luck, and more.

A full season after that second-place finish, UCLA and Dr. Holland decided to try something different—and boy did they. They offered the premier head coach position to a dancer/choreographer who had never done gymnastics.

Over the past two decades Dr. Holland has recounted the reason behind her decision many times: "I was determined to hire women as head coaches whenever the opportunity was available. When the head gymnastics coach was not performing up to expectations, I decided to not renew his contract and to look for a woman head coach. Not one woman applied for the position. I was aware of Valorie's ability with people and liked her relationship with the athletes. She was firm with them but in a strong and healthy communicative manner. I was greatly impressed by this and decided she was the right person."

Needless to say, the gymnastics community, nationwide, was up in arms and let UCLA know they thought the university had made a "ludicrous hire." Dr. Holland had been prepared for some push-back, just not at the level that poured in. She received multiple letters, phone calls, and in-person visits, all of which questioned and strongly opposed me being given the position. I had no idea of the volume of opposition coming in regarding my fitness for the head coaching job. If I had known, I would have said, "Yep, yep, yep," and agreed with all the concerns.

When I accepted the job, I told Dr. Holland I'd take it for one year to give UCLA time to find a qualified coach. In the meantime, I got busy studying successful coaches from many different sports. In my mind a coach was tough-minded, tough-talking, unwavering, intimidating, and had a dictator-like swagger. Since I had grown up on the dance stage "acting" out different characters, I figured I could act like a coach if I studied some of them well enough. So I assumed the posture of a relentless intimidating coach and learned to say things like "Go hard or go home" and "Winners make adjustments and losers make excuses." I thought these were brilliant, even though they didn't resonate with me. "Go hard or go home" wasn't something I had ever heard in a ballet studio and there were no winners or losers onstage.

To help facilitate my new position, I hired Scott Bull, an accomplished and experienced coach as my co-head coach (we had previously worked together at UCLA when I was an assistant). The night before the national championships that first year I felt like I needed to have all the answers. I had crafted my pregame speech to have real theatrical flair and pulled out my Acting 101 abilities. I started my speech echoing the same ol' things they'd all heard before, wanting them to think they would know the next words out of my mouth. Then with a carefully timed dramatic pause I cut the speech and proudly proclaimed, "That's all nonsense, it is a new era for UCLA gymnastics, now let's go win this thing." I was so concerned about performing my "role" well I didn't consider consulting my co-head coach, Scott, asking him how *we* wanted to address the team the night before the championship. The speech flopped and so did we. With my newfound manufactured "coach's attitude" and experienced support system around me, the team finished dead last that year at the NCAA championships, eight places lower than the previous year.

When we returned from the meet, I walked into Dr. Holland's office and said, "Remember I told you I was going to take the job for only one year? I want another year." A competitiveness I didn't even know I had in me had kicked in.

Dr. Holland sat there with a smug smile and nodded. She must have been thinking, "Valorie will eventually grow into this job. Hopefully sooner than later."

I studied harder. I became more hard-nosed. I demanded more of our team, learned more cutting quips, implemented sarcasm as a real stinger, and did my best to be unrelenting, unwavering, and "right" at all times. Head coaches needed to show strength by always being *right*, right?

At the beginning of that competition season we traveled to Oregon State for a meet. As a team we were pretty good, but my leadership was horrible. My competitive juices were flowing in the locker room and I was trying to wrap my head around the close loss we had just suffered when I heard the pop of gum behind me. All the girls knew we had a no gum rule on the team. Without turning around to see who had popped their gum I yelled in my new head coach vernacular, "Spit the gum out of your *#&$@* mouth!"

To be honest I knew what I said was wrong, but I wasn't sure why. Didn't other great coaches use vulgarity all the time? It later dawned on me that it wasn't the vulgarity that was the worst offense, but the fact I had placed the vulgarity on our athlete and not on the gum. That incident has always stuck with me and later when I had the opportunity to see that athlete again, I apologized.

After my second season as head coach the results were crystal clear—we were horrible and getting worse. We failed to even make it to the national championships.

That was it. I decided to resign. I remember not being upset by this and clearly thinking that I just wasn't cut out to be a coach and I should vacate the position for someone to take over who was more qualified. Then, I could go get a job doing something else in which I could truly be successful. I was actually quite excited to meet with Dr. Holland and say, "See, I told you I wasn't right for the job."

I was walking through the UCLA Student Union on my way to Dr. Holland's office to resign when I spotted one of John Wooden's books, *They Call Me Coach*. I have to admit I didn't really know much about the legendary coach at that point in time. I knew he had won a lot of championships and there was his Pyramid of Success a lot of people thought was impressive, but that was about it. I honestly don't know why I never thought to study Coach Wooden. Part of it might be that he wasn't a colorful, exciting personality, and so I thought I wouldn't have anything to glean from him because my paradigm of a great head coach included being charismatic and captivating. Oh, yes, I had a lot to learn!

I picked up the book and the first page I opened to was Coach Wooden's definition of success:

Success is peace of mind, which is a direct result of self-satisfaction in knowing you did your best to become the best you are capable of becoming.

I thought, that's weird. I had been studying very successful coaches and most of them talked about winning. Why didn't Coach Wooden talk about winning? He had won 10 NCAA basketball championships in 12 years. (In 2009 Coach Wooden was named the greatest coach in American sports history by *Sporting News*— beating out the legendary Vince Lombardi.)

I read it again.

Success is peace of mind…

No. Success is achieving a title, earning the level of income you want, winning, and earning medals. It's something tangible.

I read it again. And again. Each time I read it, the word "you" kept getting bigger and bolder and brighter. I finally got it. I realized I had been trying to be someone else. And I also realized that whenever you try to be someone else you will always be a second rate them and worse, you will never become a first rate you. With one sentence Coach Wooden humanized the process of sport for me and lifted the burden of outcome.

I went back to my office, sat at my desk, and thought, "What is it that *I* can bring to this job that is worthwhile, authentic, and inspiring?" As a dancer I knew about discipline, focus, and how to block out pain (pointe shoes are mini-torture devices). I knew what it was like to grow up in a leotard and have body image issues. I knew what it was like to be judged by how I looked. Most of all I knew how to prepare well enough to be calm and confident, vibrant and enthusiastic onstage. I *never* experienced stage fright or nervousness while waiting in the wings. And when I screwed up, which I did royally a handful of times, I knew I had to compose myself and *finish*.

I realized this is exactly what gymnasts need to learn. The biggest difference between dancers and gymnasts is that for gymnasts the feeling of satisfaction often requires a win, a ring, or a medal. To make things more complicated, in gymnastics scores are determined by other human beings, the judges. My definition of success as a dancer was being able to go onstage with confidence, knowing I was prepared. It was that simple.

I decided that would be exactly my ultimate goal in training our gymnasts. At that moment, right when I was on my way to quit, I realized I could actually do this job, and do it well. In fact, the art of preparing young women to be calm and confident before they compete is something I knew I could do as well as any other gymnastics coach. I just needed to block out all of the coaching "noise." I needed to start listening to my own voice and make the best decisions I could one day at a time, one step at a time, one choice at a time. I kicked my feet up on my desk and smiled because I knew I could do this job!

Chapter Four

Choosing to Motivate

"You have not taught until they have learned."

—John Wooden

A coach is a person who motivates change. Coaching is a massive responsibility. Parents, teachers, coaches—anyone who has a strong influence over the development of others, especially children—have the most important job in the world.

Overall, it's our job to motivate change: mentally, emotionally, and physically. The only reason people need coaches is to help them accomplish things they can't do on their own. I believe we could all benefit from great coaching throughout our life. In business we call it a mentor. On a couch or comfy chair it's our therapist. In the kitchen it's a dietitian.

A great coach is there to help us see things in a new light, to expose us to new techniques and ideas. To expose us to new language that helps us see a situation differently. To show us possibilities that can become realities if we choose to make the change.

Ahh, sports. One of the greatest venues to learn life lessons. The arts are wonderful, but they don't develop team building or encourage the competitiveness that I believe we all innately have. When I began coaching, I quickly learned that I have a very competitive spirit and, like most of us, I hate to lose. I also intrinsically knew that there had to be something more to sports than just being able to say, "Ha-ha, we beat you!" regardless of the fact that winning is really fun!

To feel good about being a coach I knew there had to be more to this leadership position than bragging rights and acquiring trophies. Sport encompasses strengthening the mind, body, and spirit. Sport develops emotional stamina—our character. Team sports connect us to one another, resulting in the vital realization that the rewards of accomplishing something together are far greater than anything we accomplish on our own.

From the moment I read and absorbed Coach Wooden's definition of success, my approach to coaching has always been to coach the *person* before the *athlete*. There are a ton of very successful coaches out there who feel the same way I do and who view the job as developing champions on and off the court.

Not all coaches take this approach, though. I've researched different coaching styles and philosophies and studied the coaches who have had the most success.

I've been able to define four predominant coaching styles, which can translate to the business world as well. Like with any personality assessment, every coach isn't necessarily going to fit into just one category. In fact, I would argue that most coaches are a blend of a few different styles. However, I've based my descriptions on coaches I personally know who are pure ambassadors for one particular style of coaching.

The Defeatist

These coaches are pessimists, cheerless, and uninspired. Any success they achieve is coincidental. They show up at the obligatory practice times and may put a few required office hours in before heading home to their *real* life. These coaches have no inspiration or motivation to craft a championship culture or program. They simply show up to get the paycheck. The defeatist will often use excuses as to why they don't do well. These coaches provide a total disservice to the athletes and their institutions. Quite often a defeatist coach will offer quips like "They don't pay me enough to want to put more into my job"; "Maybe if they gave me a bigger budget, we'd do better"; or "We can't compete with the bigger schools with more money and more desirable locations, so what's the point of busting my butt to compete with them?"

The most irksome excuse I've heard is from coaches from other universities who say they can't compete against UCLA in recruiting because we're a "sexy school." What? That is such an insult to me, as I've always done the hard work in recruiting to make sure I leave no stone unturned. Every school has its pros and cons; it's my job as a head coach to get recruits to see the exciting opportunities in our program, on our campus, and in our community.

I believe that true defeatist coaches would actually be much happier and more successful in another profession. I know of one such used-to-be-coach who is now in the tech world and is thriving in his new career. He's a totally different person now that he's found something he loves doing.

The Narcissist (Egoist)

In a narcissist's mind, the team and the athletes exist merely as the pieces needed to facilitate a reason for the narcissist's reign. You might be able to recognize a narcissist by the fact they constantly refer to "*My* team," "*My* athletes," "*My* program." While it's easy to get caught up in this verbiage, I've always been cognizant that I am a steward of UCLA. It's not *my* team, it's UCLA's team.

Narcissist coaches don't see things from anyone's point of view except their own. I witnessed one of the most egregious examples of this while I was on a recruiting trip. I was in a hotel lobby getting breakfast, and in front of me was a group of junior high school–aged boys in their soccer uniforms. They were obviously fueling up to play a game that day. Their coach came in, cut in front of all of us waiting in line, looked at the boys, and flippantly said, "Good morning, ladies." That insensitive remark deflated the boys' energy and changed the demeanor of each and every one of them. They muttered a weak and obligatory good morning back to their coach.

I was FURIOUS! Not only was that remark simply thoughtless and cruel, but what coach actually thinks calling a group of young boys—or girls for that matter—"ladies" is going to fire them up to go compete? It took everything I had not to tell off the coach and then give the boys a pep talk. (You may be wondering if I call our athletes "Ladies." I don't. They're Bruins.)

A coach being kind and courteous to their athletes is often given a bad rap as being soft and not exhibiting behavior worthy of a strong leader. Sadly, this bleeds into how coaches treat their athletes. I'm firmly of the belief that some of the strongest characteristics we can model for our malleable athletes are kindness, respect, humility, and grace. They know we're tough. They know we can demand them to work hard. They know we can be relentless. However, when we show them respect, it carries far more weight than when we just bark orders at them.

That respect is most evident when an athlete *doesn't* perform well. Too often in our sport, we see a coach walk away when an athlete makes a mistake, sometimes even before the routine is completed. What message does that send to the athlete? "You're not worthy of my attention unless you compete well." This is the action of a narcissist. The focus is on them and not on the athlete.

The Strategist

A *pure* strategist focuses on the fundamentals of the game and not on the athletes. They absolutely love the sport, and they put the majority of their effort into formulating a winning plan. Then they tend to work the plan from a clipboard, whiteboard, and film. All great coaches are strategists. They have to be able to craft an innovative plan.

Martha Karolyi, the former US national team women's gymnastics coordinator, is a brilliant strategist. She and her husband, Bela, developed a battleground to train athletes to be indestructible athletic robots with impenetrable shields that made them impervious to all pain, just as they had done in Romania before coming to the States. Martha and Bela have also been accused of excessive verbal and emotional abuse of the athletes they trained. They have been accused of forcing injured athletes—some hurt quite severely—to keep training. Martha will argue that she was not abusive at all, insisting instead that everything she did only made the athletes "stronger." The athletes will admit to being part of the most indestructible gymnastics army in the world, but that came at an extremely high price, which included broken bodies and emotional scars.

Betty Okino was a 1992 Olympic bronze medalist who trained with Bela and Martha before Martha became the national team coordinator. She doesn't dispute that the Karolyis developed athletic champions, but she also contends that in the process the athletes were stripped of any sense of self and self-worth. The young women who trained with the Karolyis did not develop the necessary tools to deal with life after they left the dictator regime, and the limelight and all the attention disappeared. Betty echoed what a lot of the elite athletes I have coached have described: when you are no longer one of the top athletes, when you are no longer needed, you are "discarded." While there was a coldness to the training environment at the Karolyi Ranch (the former elite program training center on the Karolyi property about 60 miles north of Houston), there is a "nothingness" after your time there is done. Betty said, "No one cares about you in 'the after.' It's in 'the after' that you realize they never cared about you as a person, only for the medals you could win. That is a pain that is so deep you don't even know how to find words to describe it. No one from USAG sees the emptiness that is felt in 'the after' except the athletes and then later their college coaches."

To be truly great strategists, coaches must be able to craft an innovative, winning plan. And there are as many ways to do that as there are coaches.

Coach Al Scates was the UCLA men's volleyball coach for 48 years, during which time the team won 19 championships. One of his strategies was that he only paid attention to the top 14–16 athletes on the team. The other 10 were literally "behind the curtain." There was a curtain in the practice gym that divided the space. If you were in the top 16, you practiced on one side of the curtain with Coach Scates. If you weren't in the top 16, you practiced on the other side of the curtain, in a smaller space, with an assistant coach or team manager until you performed your way into the top 16.

UCLA's current head women's volleyball coach, Mike Sealy, was one of Coach Scates's athletes. He told me, "The simple reason Coach Scates's system was so effective was because it literally was Darwinism, survival of the fittest." He went on to explain that one of the most impressive things about this system was "just because an athlete might not get optimal coaching and playing time didn't diminish their ability to achieve greatness. There were two athletes on our team that never made it to the top 16 side of the curtain and yet, because of their constant drive to *want* to get to the other side of the curtain, they went on to play in the Olympic Games." This system not only honed one's competitive fibers, it weeded out the lazy, the whiners, the weak. This system rewarded perseverance and grit. One never knew when one of the top 16 might be injured and you'd be called to the other side of the curtain. This was what you prepared for. Your one shot to show that you've prepared, are ready, and will never go back behind the curtain.

Think what you will of this method, it worked for Coach Scates; he's the all-time winningest men's volleyball coach in NCAA history.

Anson Dorrance, the legendary University of North Carolina women's soccer coach with 21 NCAA championships under his belt, is also someone I consider to be a great strategist. Anson perfected a training system called the Competitive Cauldron, which was first developed by yet another strategist, legendary UNC basketball coach Dean Smith. With the Competitive Cauldron, everything an athlete does in training and in competition counts.

As Coach Dorrance explains, every day in training the team managers keep track of everything every athlete does. At the end of the training day, all of the athletes can see where they rank in comparison to their teammates. The purpose of the Cauldron is to ignite a competitive fire among the athletes. The Cauldron stresses to the athletes the importance that every little thing matters. The Cauldron inevitably invites each athlete to fight their way to the top of the team stats, which creates an intense and healthy competitive battleground.

Coach Dorrance took Dean Smith's idea of the Competitive Cauldron and tweaked it to best suit his team. The Competitive Cauldron is known to work so well that in the NFL, in 2013, Coach Pete Carroll took the model and tweaked it for the Seattle Seahawks. The next year the Seahawks won the Super Bowl.

I think the Competitive Cauldron is a brilliant strategy because it teaches accountability, and athletes quickly learn that everything they do in sports—as in life—matters.

We actually implement mini-Competitive Cauldrons almost every day of training. In order to get most of the athletes to participate, we always include a simple skill, something like a simple round-off, back handspring, layout back flip to a stuck landing, ending with a controlled salute. Each athlete gets a score for the first round and then they line up from lowest to highest score. Then the fun begins. We move on to head-to-head battle. An athlete can choose to challenge another athlete for their spot by performing the skill again. If their second score is higher than the score of the athlete they challenge, the two switch places in the line.

I love how feisty the athletes get during this challenge. There is not a lot of head-to-head competition in gymnastics, so implementing challenges like this strengthens the athletes' competitive drive.

At the same time, it shows them that it's good to challenge and beat out a teammate because it all helps make the team stronger as a whole.

A true strategist is brilliant and a consummate student of the game and of sport. A true strategist embraces the facts/stats and crafts a training plan that encourages each athlete to want to beat their fellow teammate, knowing it's only making the team better. A true strategist understands and is precise in implementing the biblical phrase "iron sharpens iron."

The problem with *only* caring about the strategy of the win is that it takes the human element out of the equation. Coaching this way becomes a missed opportunity to teach athletes unbreakable life mores and skills that would help make them strong individuals and strong leaders. Sports help produce super-humans who can help make the world a better place. Do we really think that a shiny gold object is going to impact fellow mankind positively? Who cares how many medals Michael Phelps (insert any athletic superstar's name) earns if he doesn't use his fame and influence for the greater good? That's the whole essence of sport—to develop leaders and life champions who transcend the game.

The Altruist

An altruist is selfless and devoted to others. Altruists are mentors who treat athletes as people who are interested in learning how to live better lives through sport. The altruist will "take the higher road" and lead at certain points through intuition, emotional quotient, and compassion. Altruists understand that everything they say or do will be taken in and translated by their athletes in some fashion. Altruists will always first consider the needs of their athletes or coaches under their leadership before their own comfort and ego.

The "perfect" coach would be a combination of a strong strategist, altruist, and yes, narcissist (egoist). I add the last one because, as long as a coach has a strong acumen for the sport, a strategic plan for getting the athletes to reach competitive greatness and a comprehensive *healthy* embodiment of what success and winning mean, the ego doesn't get in the way and can provide a healthy dose of confidence and swagger to the program.

In retrospect, I believe our success at UCLA has come from the fact that I understand I am *not* the "perfect" coach and therefore have taken great care to assemble a "complete" coaching staff—one that embodies all of the positive attributes of great coaches. I naturally gravitate toward the altruist and yet, with a lot of dialogue with our coaching staff, I've learned how to be a good strategist.

Ultimately, how we coach is 100% our choice. Our coaching style is not solely based on our innate personalities. Our job is to be extremely mindful of what we say and do. Everything matters.

Every good coach knows that *magic* happens when the whole person is vibrant—when an athlete gets "in the zone." If you only coach the fundamentals or execution of skills, that's all you'll get back. To be clear, you can develop athletic champions this way. You can win championships this way. The highest levels of competition across all sports are filled with these coach–athlete combos. To get the magic, however, you need to strengthen what's happening on the inside. For *magic* to happen, you need trust. There needs to be trust between you and the athlete; an athlete needs to trust themselves; and there needs to be trust between teammates. When the strength of trust is palpable, you're no longer solely concerned with execution and instead can be receptive to the connectivity of *magic*.

Trying to get a group of people to do what you want is really difficult. Getting them to *want* to do those things is even harder and takes a lot more effort than leading through dictatorship. When I'm frustrated, I come back to the ultimate goal of a coach: *to motivate change* mentally, emotionally, physically.

We all need to embrace our intrinsic style of coaching and leading, otherwise we become fake and unauthentic. However, a constant assessment of self and how we affect those in our care can only heighten our ability to motivate and lead.

Chapter Five

Coaches Who Inspire, Break Barriers

"Dreams and dedication are a powerful combination."

—William Longgood

U p until 1986 there was only one collegiate team that had won a national championship in NCAA women's gymnastics—that was the University of Utah led by Greg Marsden. In 1987 Georgia broke the Utes' streak and won their first championship under the leadership of Suzanne Yoculan. A year later Alabama broke into the winner's circle under head coach Sarah Patterson. For the next decade those were the only three teams to win a team championship. In 1997 UCLA finally won our first championship.

Greg, Suzanne, and Sarah are legends in our gymnastics world. Each of them is extremely unique in their coaching style and yet each is hugely successful, in figuring out not only how to win but also how to put over 10,000 fans in the stands. Up until each of them retired, their arenas were sold out for all of their home meets.

Greg Marsden is the unequivocal godfather of collegiate gymnastics. In the early 1980s, when college gymnastics was just emerging as an NCAA sport, Utah's fan base was rapidly growing to ultimately sold-out crowds. I picked Greg's brain constantly about how to better market the UCLA program to build our fan base. Greg would give away 100,000 tickets per meet hoping for a 10 percent return.

UCLA's marketing department didn't want to give away free tickets because they didn't want to "dilute" our "product." I remember being so frustrated that I asked our marketing director, someone I otherwise really enjoy working with, why we weren't doing what Greg was doing since he had been proven, over and over again, that it worked. We never did agree on an answer. To this day, Greg remains one of the most innovative voices in our sport.

As for Suzanne Yoculan, she never hides what she thinks and makes no apologies for speaking her truth, which quite often caused a stir because she was so transparent with how she felt. The biggest thing I learned from Suzanne is that just because I'm a head coach, it doesn't mean I'm supposed to have all the answers. It *does* mean that if something isn't working, then it's my job to figure out how to change that. I remember the 2004 NCAA championship, we had just won our fourth title in five years. After Suzanne congratulated me, she said something that scared the pants off me: "Val, I am so sick and tired of losing to you." That one sentence scared me because I knew it meant she was about to do something drastically different in order for her team to start winning again.

She did just that. In 2005 Suzanne moved her entire team into a house right outside the university's campus. The *entire* team *had* to live together. I remember being so excited about this, at first, because it seemed inevitable to me that 15 girls all living and training together was a guaranteed recipe for disaster. There was *no way* it would work. Nope, it worked brilliantly. It not only brought the team really close together (in every way!), but from what I understand they held each other accountable for everything. Georgia went on to win the next *five* championships before we grabbed another one in 2010.

However, by the spring of 2016, when we hadn't won another championship, I told our coaching staff that we needed to take a page out of Suzanne's book: if we wanted a different result we had to do something differently. Our biggest issue was what our student-athletes were doing outside the gym that affected their performances inside the gym (things like bad eating habits, staying up too late, etc.); we needed to find a way to make them at least think twice about their choices. So, for the first time in UCLA gymnastics history, I decided to room all of our freshmen together. Guess what… it worked. We didn't win the championship in 2017, but that year we didn't have the clichéd freshman weight gain, I didn't hear of any partying issues, and we had far better academic reports from the girls' teachers and tutors—and it set the stage for even more improvement the next year.

From Sarah Patterson, I learned how to become a massive presence in our community, cultivating sponsors, donors, and fans at the grassroots level. In 2004 she was the first collegiate athletic coach of any sport to start the Pink Meet in support of Breast Cancer Awareness. She got the entire city of Tuscaloosa involved in that event each year. When I inquired about what she did and how she went about it, Sarah sent me an entire folder of everything she did to promote that meet and cause.

All of us who love collegiate gymnastics will be forever grateful for the trails blazed in and out of the gym by these three. I can't even begin to imagine where we would be today if Greg, Suzanne, and Sarah hadn't had the collective vision of seeing women's gymnastics as a premier collegiate sport. Today, women's gymnastics consistently has the third highest ratings on college sports TV networks, surpassed only by men's basketball and football. Not only did Greg, Suzanne, and Sarah see a future of packed arenas and sky-high TV ratings, but they had the determination to put their innovative ideas into action. They laid the foundation for the rest of us coaches to use as a blueprint for success.

Through their relentless quest for more fans, higher ratings, and more championships they challenged the rest of us to figure out how to find that same success in our own unique collegiate environments. This was a perfect example of learning from the masters but tweaking my recipe for success at UCLA, using ingredients that would resonate best in a culture like Los Angeles versus Salt Lake City, Athens, or Tuscaloosa.

As I've already said, I've had no greater teacher than UCLA basketball coach John Wooden. But, as strange as it may seem, in 1998 I had been at UCLA for 16 years, had been employing Coach Wooden's philosophies about coaching for roughly half that time, and yet I had never been formally introduced to him!

Coach Wooden had been retired since 1975. Even so, he was still very much a presence on campus. My husband, Bobby Field, arrived at UCLA in 1978 where he coached football for us for 22 years before moving into athletic administration. On his very first day on campus, Bobby went to his locker after working out and stopped cold. The great Coach Wooden was getting stuff out of the locker right next to his! Welcome to UCLA, Bobby!

Bobby and I got married in 1998. We had been married for just a few months when I asked him to call Coach Wooden and invite him over for dinner. Yes, I could have made the call but thought it made better sense if someone Coach knew called.

Bobby responded, "My love, Coach Wooden is in such demand and the last thing he needs is another obligation on his calendar. I'm really not comfortable calling and asking him to do this."

I took a deep breath because my husband is the epitome of polite, but I thought, "Why would Coach look at this as an obligation? He can always say 'no.'"

This conversation between me and my husband replayed every night for three weeks. I was a broken record. To every reason Bobby gave me for not calling I countered with "He can always say 'no.'" It worked…it took a while, but it worked.

To shut me up, Bobby acquiesced and dialed Coach's number.

Bobby: Coach, I don't know if you know this, but I'm married to Valorie Kondos, our gymnastics coach. She really wants to meet you and was wondering if you might be up for coming over for dinner. I told her how busy your schedule is and we totally understand if you can't make it.

Coach: Bobby, you're confusing me. Are you inviting me to dinner or are you telling me why I can't come?

Bobby: Coach, of course we want you to come to dinner, but I just wanted to let you know…

Coach: Bobby, stop right there! If you're asking me to come to dinner, the answer is yes, I would love to have dinner with you and Valorie.

So, Coach came over for dinner that night and many, many nights after. That initial dinner started a friendship between us that grew closer with each passing year until the day he died. When I think back to how our relationship materialized, it was as simple as me nagging Bobby to pick up the phone and make the ask.

Dreams are a dime a dozen in life. Those rewarded are the ones who execute—even when it's as simple as picking up a phone—just as I did in getting to UCLA and now through Bobby to launch one of the most meaningful relationships I've had in my life.

The "art of the Ask" is one of the most important skills to master in choreographing your life. The first big Ask I remember was in 1976 when I called up Jim Stephenson of AgileLites to see if they needed a dance coach. He didn't. Instead he learned that I played the piano and hired me to play for floor exercise routines. Even though I wasn't hired to coach dance, that single ask launched me into this brand-new world of gymnastics.

My next big Ask came in 1982 when I called up Jerry Tomlinson, the head coach of the UCLA gymnastics team and asked if they needed a dance coach. My entire 38-year career at UCLA all started with that Ask. Had I not had the confidence to make that call none of my UCLA experiences would have happened.

Outside of coaching, I've had an illustrious side career directing and choreographing live shows at venues including Disneyland, SeaWorld, the San Diego Zoo, and the unveiling of Kareem Abdul Jabbar's statue at Staples Center. This all started in 1989 when I asked Jerry Tomlinson's wife, Donna, who was in charge of the character department at Disneyland, how I could audition to be one of their choreographers. Donna gave me a contact in the entertainment department that within a few months led me to my very first choreography job outside of crafting gymnastics floor routines. Since that time I have been choreographing and/or directing SeaWorld

San Diego's "human shows." One show I choreographed, called *Riptide*, won an IAAPA (International Association of Amusement Parks and Attractions) award, the highest honor for a theme park show.

This all came about because I wasn't afraid to *ask*. What's the worst thing that could have happened in each of those circumstances? They could have said no.

It's crucially important to know *how* to ask. Asking something of someone is in essence asking for a favor. Here are some of what I consider to be essential qualities of an effective ask: know what you're asking for before you make the call; have your request be succinct and clear; and be gracious, humble, and appreciative, without being apologetic, obsequious, or bullish.

Once you've been given an answer—whether or not it's what you were hoping to hear—be sure to keep your response short. If you've gotten a favorable response then simply say something like "Thank you for this opportunity, I look forward to working together." If you've gotten an unfavorable response, don't argue. The person doesn't owe you any explanation as to why they are turning down your request. Importantly, you *will* have another opportunity to ask again, at some later date, provided you are not argumentative in response to the initial rejection.

After the Ask comes the Nudge. Why do you need the Nudge if the person said yes? Well, just because someone has agreed to do something, even if they have the best of intentions, it doesn't mean they'll remember to do it.

The "art of the Nudge" lies at the heart of tenacity. A properly timed and well-executed Nudge can be quite rewarding. The nuances of the nudge are crucial to intuit and master. The best way for me to figure out how to nudge someone is to put myself in the other person's shoes and try to figure out how I would want to be nudged. It usually sounds something like "Hello, I imagine you've been swamped…I was wondering if you've been able to give more thought to what we discussed?"

Remember, the person receiving the nudge usually doesn't owe you a thing. If you come off like you are entitled to having the person follow through with what they agreed to and doing that on *your* timeline, then you can easily send them into withdrawal mode. They could choose to say, "Sorry, I'm just not going to be able to help you out with this." They don't need to give you a single reason, you simply ticked them off. Your time and their time are both important, which gets us to the Drop. If you've gotten an initial no or are not getting a response to your Nudge, there comes a time when it's best to drop the issue for the time being. That doesn't mean you can't revisit it at a later date, it just means the timing is not good now, and more often than not there is nothing you can do to change that.

What I've also learned from being on both sides of the Ask and the Nudge is that if the issue is dropped for a while, then the next time it is brought up and discussed, both parties usually come to the table with a fresh perspective.

Among the many things I learned from my mom—and the list is long!—was another communication technique focusing on the importance of concise, firm communication aptly called the "Broken Record." This is something I love to share with our student-athletes. It helped me understand that I have a voice, my opinions count, and I have a choice which, once I make it, should be respected.

I remember being in high school when my mom was reading *When I Say No, I Feel Guilty,* by Manuel J. Smith. One day, when my friends were over, my mom said to us, "OK girls, I'm going to teach you the art of the Broken Record."

What? My friends and I couldn't begin to imagine what she was talking about. She continued, "It's how to be a respectful broken record. Respectful to yourself and respectful to whom you're talking."

She then read out loud to us from the book. The Broken Record technique is "a skill that by calm repetition—saying what you want over and over again—teaches persistence without you having to rehearse arguments or angry feelings beforehand, in order to be 'up' for dealing with others."

The key here is to know what you want and to stick to it by communicating in a way that does not give the other person any opening to question your choices. I have employed the Broken Record technique many times over the years when I don't feel I need to explain my choice. I come up with a short, standard line and repeat it over and over until the person stops bugging me. I don't engage in any argument they want to have, don't veer off the choice I have made into any side discussion, and simply stick to and repeat my response. The result is that the other person has no option but to eventually concede and move on.

I use the following Broken Record example with our athletes because I know what I'm describing is probably relevant—and therefore, helpful—to a lot of them.

When I was in my early 20s, I was on a date with a guy who had asked me out to dinner. I met him at the Chart House in Malibu. We had a lovely time. After dinner I said, "Thank you. I had a great time." I then proceeded to approach my car to go home.

He stopped me before I could get into my car and said, "Wait, my apartment is not far. Why don't you come over for a drink?"

Instantly, I knew I was going to need to use my Broken Record skills.

Me (smiling): Thank you for dinner. I had a great time. I'm going to go home now.

Him: Why don't you come over for one drink?

Me (thinking while still smiling): You asked me to dinner, and I agreed. You didn't ask me to nor did I ever agree to go to your apartment for a drink.

Me (smiling): Thank you for dinner. I had a great time. I'm going to go home now.

Him: What? Do you have to get up early? It's not even 10 o'clock.

Me (thinking and still smiling): It's none of your business whether I have to get up early or not.

Me: Thank you for dinner. I had a great time. I'm going to go home now.

Him (now annoyed): Just give me one good reason why you can't come over for a half an hour. Do you have to get up early?

Me (thinking): Seriously? I owe him an explanation?

Me (trying to keep smiling but now I think it's more of a smirk and I'm okay with that): Thank you for dinner. I had a great time. I'm going to go home now.

Him (pissed off): I don't get it. It's just a half hour.

Me (forget the smile and the smirk; returning the pissed off tone): Thank you for dinner. I had a great time. I'm going to go home now.

Him (JACKASS): Yeah, I heard you the previous 20 times you said that. I can't believe I bought you dinner and this is all I get.

Me (to myself, not really surprised): WHATTTTT? Ahh, the truth comes out. Stay calm. Breathe. Choose your next move carefully.

Me (calmly and speaking a tad more slowly): Thank you for dinner. I had a great time. I'm going to go home now.

When I share this story with the girls, their first reaction is that they can't believe I actually did that. But when I get to the part where they hear the truth about what he was really thinking, they see the beauty of the Broken Record. Had I given in and said, "Okay, I'll come over for a half hour for one drink," or had I felt the need to give him an excuse as to why I couldn't come over would have set up a further, higher-stakes chess match of wills. I knew my checkmate move, and I chose to take it right at the start.

The point is you don't owe anyone more of an explanation for why you do or don't want to do something other than, "I just don't want to." There's no reason to feel compelled to give a fuller or "better" excuse. The honest and therefore most respectful excuse is usually "Thank you for the invite, but I don't want to."

Unfortunately, being that blunt is tough for a lot of people to accept—even when you are being respectfully blunt. I don't know why that should be the case. Wouldn't you want someone to be honest rather than tell you something that you strongly suspect—or worse, just know—is made up?

The Broken Record is so effective because you are listening to someone's request and replying sincerely, respectfully, and honestly. When I use this technique, most people will simply move on, or at worst be a bit confused and ask a follow-up question. Rarely, at least in my experience, do they get pissed off like that long ago date. And if they do, I quickly realize they're coming from their perspective, which happens to be different than mine. No need for either of us to prove the other wrong, it's just time to respectfully move on.

Chapter Six

A Peek Inside My Playbook

"Self-awareness is probably the most important thing towards being a champion."

—Billie Jean King

One of the top selling T-shirts in our student union says, "What would Coach Wooden do?" I have to admit that for years, because Coach was my greatest mentor, I felt like I needed to try to be like him. I had to keep reminding myself of the mistakes I made when I first became a head coach and tried to mimic others.

As I'm writing this I'm chuckling because my husband is *a lot* like Coach Wooden. I have said many times over the course of our marriage, "It is *so hard* to be married to someone *so good*!" For the first few years of our marriage I kept trying to be as "good" as my husband; not only an impossible task but also extremely frustrating, restrictive, annoying, and infuriating. One day I was in a particularly immature mood when I said to Bobby, "Don't you ever get sick of me?" With his saintly nature he replied, "My Love, I chose to marry *you*. The good and the brat. I don't want you to be like me, otherwise I would have married someone more like me."

I will always remember after we won our fifth NCAA championship, the *Los Angeles Times* wrote an article about Coach Wooden and me. At one point the reporter said to me, "You're becoming the next John Wooden." Before I could guffaw and tell him how ridiculous that was, Coach spoke up and said, "Why would she want to be another John Wooden when she can be a great Valorie Kondos Field?" I will forever remember that moment as a rite of passage to once and for all stop trying to be like others and just focus on being the best me I can be.

So how do you improve yourself through the inspiration of others while still being true to you? I learned to embrace a shift in my mindset to Act As If.

Most of us already have a story we're living by, but it's *unconscious*. When you Act As If you take control and make your story *conscious*, even if you don't feel it's your default mode at that moment. Acting as if is a powerful tool that can put you in a position to gain experience and knowledge until you no longer need to act and instead can simply *be*. The more colloquial way to say this is "fake it until you make it."

I first incorporated this philosophy when I was 18 years old, dancing and struggling with finding the perfect diet, when I made the decision to stop thinking of myself as an overweight dancer who needed to lose weight. Instead, I started to think of myself as a lean, fit, "heath nut." It was remarkable how quickly my habits changed from sneaking chips and overeating to only eating when I was hungry and then only eating healthy food (most of the time). Part of what helped me was to observe the habits of people I felt were really fit. I found that they ate slowly; they weren't obsessed with food when it was around; and they never finished a meal. Act As If is a powerful tool. I followed their lead and gave myself a consistent internal reminder that I was a health nut. It worked.

Here are a few of my Act As If buttons that, even today, I find myself constantly pushing to reboot:

I act as if I'm super healthy. For me, this means eating clean and exercising at least a few times per week. Sorry, potato chips, as much as I love you, healthy people don't eat a whole bag in a single sitting.

I act as if I'm organized. I need a refresh and reboot on this one a lot, sometimes multiple times a day. At home, it helps that Bobby is super organized and tidy. That makes my mess an eyesore and an unavoidable reminder of the need to change my default of being a slob. Even if I only put a few things away each day, at least I'm doing something to Act As If I'm organized.

Why is being organized important to me? Because I realize that when I'm somewhat organized I spend a lot less time looking for things, get a lot less frustrated, and see what I want to accomplish daily more clearly. I can also delegate much better.

> I act as if I'm a morning person. This means planning my life so I get up early and get going, even on the weekends. It's important to stay on a schedule, which includes having a sleep pattern. This helps prevent me from feeling lethargic during the week when I do have to get up early. I also refuse to allow myself to say anything negative about "having" to getting up early. Instead, I have gotten in the habit of waking up and thinking, "Yay, I get another day."

I want to make it clear that there's a *huge* difference between acting like I can do something long enough to reap the benefits of positive behavioral change and merely being a copycat and attempting to mimic the entirety of someone else. The difference between acting as if in order to be a better version of myself versus trying to be someone I'm not, is a lesson that becomes crystal clear when I read other coaching biographies. I'm a voracious reader and I've always been fascinated to learn all of the different ways someone else has found success, and how they've sustained and oftentimes had to re-create success. I've become aware of the fact that we are all very different and need to forge our own master playbook for living, leading, and teaching. Reading how different New England Patriots coach Bill Belichick is from Seattle Seahawks coach Pete Carroll or knowing how different Suzanne Yoculan was from Greg Marsden actually encourages me to "do me."

This self-awareness is an awakening I see every year with the athletes going through our program. If there is one single truth I want them to learn it's that Life is a Choice, which starts with our thoughts. Ask any of our recent graduates and they'll recite to you the following statement: "Life is about Choice, and the choices I make will dictate the life I lead."

It's indisputable that our mind dictates our emotions, which in turn dictate our actions. I have heard many versions of this equation: "Say. Believe. Behave"; "Think. Feel. Act."; and "Think it. Speak it. Do it" to name a few. My version of this is "Say it. Know it. Own it."

When I first propose this to recruits or to our freshmen they think it's just another "Miss Val-ism." I assure them it's not my philosophy, but a *truth*.

Your brain is the most *you* there is! It's the only part of your body with a conscience. The rest of your body is mostly fluid, muscle, and bone. Unless you have a mental illness or disability, you have control over your thoughts.

The tricky part is to actually take control of your thoughts and choose to feed the good thoughts and starve the bad ones. That's where the work lies. You need to try to figure out your "why." Why do you choose to feed certain thoughts and starve others? Is there some payoff to feeding negative thoughts about ourselves or about others? Are we looking for an excuse or an out? Are we avoiding the *real* work? Are we afraid of failure? Maybe we choose to think mean things about someone else because it makes us feel better about ourselves and it's easier than doing the work of self-improvement.

It's common to lash out due to our own insecurities. However, we have a choice. Instead of feeding jealousy and making snide remarks to tear someone down, we can refocus on our own opportunities that have nothing to do with the other person. When we choose to cut down others it doesn't make us taller, it chips away at our integrity and only makes us more insecure, bitter, and spiteful.

Every year I struggle to not laugh when some of our student-athletes begin to make their excuses. They'll say things like "I couldn't study, my mind kept wandering" or "I can't help it when I go to mean girl" or "I'm just not a naturally happy person, that's why it takes me until halfway through workout to be nice." Inevitably, there are some on the team, usually freshmen, who absolutely don't want to believe they have control over their thoughts. I always do my best to keep a straight face as I start the inquisition, "Really, you can find the way to be happy at 9:00 a.m. but not at 8:00 a.m. because you're not a naturally happy person? Granted, it may take you a while to wake up, but you really can't decide to be kind and not a brat until you feel like being happy?"

"Thoughts" are what we choose to say in our mind. Thoughts trigger our emotions. This process concludes with us "owning" our actions. Regardless of right or wrong, to own your actions means you are conscious of why you chose them in the first place. Too many of us skirt the responsibility of owning our thoughts, words, and actions or don't believe they have the impact that they do. In reality, the thoughts, words, and actions we choose are the essence of who we are; ultimately, they dictate the life we lead.

There is a Native American story I love about taking responsibility for your thoughts. An aging grandfather sits with his grandson and explains that there's a great battle inside each of us between a bad wolf and a good wolf. The bad wolf grows and gets stronger with anger, fear, arrogance, greed, and bitterness. The good wolf gains strength through positive thoughts, kindness, empathy, compassion, generosity, and gratitude. The grandfather continues to describe the fight raging between the wolves. His grandson looks at him and asks, "Which wolf wins?" The grandfather replies, "The one you feed."

In Buddhism there is a concept called "fundamental darkness," which refers to the negative thoughts/energy that humans carry around with them every day. These thoughts and the energy that accompanies them are an example of how ignorance prevents enlightenment. Everyone's fundamental darkness is unique and personal.

I translate this same philosophy to Thought Bubbles. Simple, not as eerie, but just as effective. Instead of wolves or dark energy I like to offer the image that with every incident life hands us we conjure up different thoughts encased in their own bubbles. I simply starve the bubbles I don't like and feed the ones I want to encourage to grow. The point is, we have a choice in which ideas we feed and which ones we starve.

One of the most rewarding parts of coaching is when the girls come to the realization that they, in fact, *do* have a conscious choice over their thoughts. It's not just that they have a choice—people choose things all the time and fail to take responsibility—but that they *own* their choice. When they take control of their thoughts, they no longer have an "out." It can be very scary, at first, to admit that you are accountable for your actions; it puts you in uncharted emotional terrain and you can no longer play the role of a victim. However, this is the most important milestone in starting to take control of your life. While initially daunting, acknowledging that you own your thoughts is liberating and empowering.

I had the Life is about Choice conversation with a coach I worked with many years ago. As a father of four it was interesting how he interpreted this concept. He absolutely disagreed with me and vehemently said, "If someone harms my child, I'm not going to sit there and rationalize whether I go after him. I will kill him."

I thought, "Okay, but that's not what this is about." I kept trying to get him to understand it's not about choosing the "right" thought to feed or about being judged for your decision. Accepting that Life is about Choice is simply acknowledging you are in total control of your thoughts and emotions and you *own* the consequences that result.

Every choice has numerous consequences including the choice to do nothing. There's a fallacy that we can be passive and simply exist without having a ripple effect on ourselves and others. We think if we are in a bad mood, but simply minding our own business, it won't affect others around us. That's not true. This is a conversation I'm constantly having with our team. When you enter a room, you're affecting the energy either positively or negatively. It would be great if we could disappear into the background, but that's not how it works.

There have been many times during training when I'm just not feeling great, happy, or energized. I would love to come in and do my job giving technical corrections and not have to worry about how my words and actions are perceived. I'm not being mean to anyone, can't I just come in to the gym some days and "just be" without the girls or staff being negatively affected? Nope, I can't. We are a team. And just like in any social setting, whether it be with family or friends, we are responsible for our part of the emotional energy we seek to create. We can't "opt out" of our social responsibility of our behavior without owning the consequences, no matter how tired, poopy, or pissy we are.

This leads to the acknowledgement of white space or white noise in life. This is a whole other realm of responsibility—one I hadn't even considered as I embarked on my coaching career. It hit me, early on, that oftentimes what I wasn't saying was impacting our student-athletes—even when I was keeping silent for good reason.

In the late 1990s one of our best competitors was Deborah Mink. She was a rock. She always showed up ready to compete. I would let her just do her thing in competitions while choosing to spend my time helping those who needed a pep talk or needed to calm down. During her sophomore year Deborah told me it always hurt her feelings that I didn't give her much attention during meets as I spent all my time with her teammates. I was *shocked*! Didn't she know the reason I left her alone was because I did not need to worry about her? Didn't she realize that her teammates who received the most attention were the ones who needed someone to coach them up? Didn't she realize what a huge compliment it was? No! Why should she? I had never thought to fill her in on my thoughts and the reasons why I did what I did. To this day, 20 years later, I constantly think about what *I don't* say as much as what *I do* say that might impact those around me. It becomes nearly impossible to not see all the potential influence the white space (or white noise) in life has when you realize how far-reaching it can be.

One of my favorite examples of white or negative space (as it's referred to in the art world) is the FedEx logo. In branding it is one of the most revered designs of all time. It seems so very simple. Two words mashed together in purple and orange. What makes this logo so brilliant? It is the forward-pointing arrow hidden in the white space between the E and X. Once you see what's hidden in the white space, you can't unsee it. It's the same with life.

Once we truly understand the concept of "Say It. Know It. Own It." there is no turning back to the blissful state of being a "victim." We can no longer blame our poor behavior on our unruly and insensitive mind. It is an awakening that can't be reversed. I smile thinking about the poor puzzled faces of our young Bruins, and the bewilderment they feel knowing that they've crossed the line into a world without excuses.

Chapter Seven

Discovering Your Default

"Between stimulus and response, there is a space. In the space
there is the power to choose our response. In our response lies
our growth and our freedom."

—Viktor Frankl, Man's Search for Meaning

The difference between being conscious of our thoughts and
being unconscious is the difference between *responding* and
reacting. It's a pause. It's a breath. It's being mindful of our thoughts,
which leads to a considered and intentional response.

When we *react* we don't slow down to analyze and make a
choice. It's reflexive and dips into our fears, biases, and current emotions. Reacting can be an innate part of our personality or it can be
learned. Reacting doesn't necessarily mean you're taking the wrong

action, but you're not owning the choice. I find when I *respond* I have far less regret than when I simply react to something.

One of my favorite things we do with our team each year is have them take a personality assessment test. I know a few psychologists who don't adhere to the psychology behind personality assessments. They believe that personality assessment tests like the DISC, the Myers-Briggs assessment, or the Enneagram put people in a box and absolve them from owning responsibility for their thoughts, emotions, and actions. I believe just the opposite. I believe these tests help each of us find our default, or our natural inclination on how we *react* to things. Once we know that, we can be more mindful in *choosing* how we *respond*.

In 2009 I had been a head coach for 19 years and felt I needed a psychological facelift. I was sick of hearing myself spew the same things to our team year after year. So I contacted Dr. Foster Mobley, a highly successful leadership coach whose clients have included Citicorp, Deloitte, Disney, and Nokia, among others. I introduced myself and then I unabashedly explained that although we had won five national championships, we had never won three in a row and I hadn't led our team to an NCAA championship title in five years, and I wanted his help in seeing if I was the reason. In an interview with my coauthor Steve "Coop" Cooper, Foster said, "I've never had a leader before or since come to me with that degree of vulnerability, candor, courage, or directness."

Foster then asked me about my vision for our program and from there we spent many hours discussing the qualities of an effective leader.

During that initial conversation, Foster asked if I'd take a personality assessment test called the Enneagram, which is based on the ancient wisdom of numerous religions and philosophies. I agreed to do it, partly because I love this stuff and having already taken the Myers-Briggs and DISC, I was curious to see if another assessment would reveal the same traits.

The test breaks personality types into nine descriptions, which are identified by numbers (I've consolidated the following definitions using two books on the Enneagram: *The Enneagram: A Christian Perspective* by Richard Rohr, and *The Complete Enneagram* by Beatrice Chestnut, PhD):

1. **The Reformer:** They need to be perfect. Ones are idealists, motivated and driven by longing for a true, just, and moral world. They have a teacher mentality that reflects an unconscious need for superiority.

2. **The Helper:** They need to be needed. They impart a measure of acceptance and appreciation that can help others believe in their own value. They are upbeat, driven, energetic, and friendly, especially in the service of others or with projects they feel passionate about. They can also be martyrs, sacrificing their own needs and desires to win over others, but then suffering for it. (I'm a *Two*.)

3. **The Achiever:** They need to succeed. Threes draw their life energy from succeeding. They appear to accomplish things with ease and assurance but are fueled by an unwavering drive to succeed/win. They are also very image conscious. They focus their attention on tasks and goals to create an image of success in the eyes of others. Threes identify with their work, believing they are what they do, and can lose touch with who they really are.

4. **The Individualist:** They need to be special. They are highly sensitive and almost always artistically gifted. Fours are generally afraid of conflict, will work tirelessly when they feel passionately connected to something, and can see what's missing and speak to it.

5. **The Investigator:** They need to perceive. Fives believe knowledge is power, so they like to observe what's going on around them without getting too involved, especially emotionally. Fives live in their heads and often detach from their emotions.

6. **The Loyalist:** They need security. They are cooperative, team players, and reliable. In relationships one can count on their fidelity; they are extremely loyal. They express the passion of fear through a need for protection, for friendship, and for banding together with others.

7. **The Enthusiast:** They need to avoid pain. They express idealism and enthusiasm as a way of making themselves

feel active and valued in the world. They are quick to alter a course because they frequently imagine something better than ordinary reality.

8. **The Challenger:** They need to be against. They are strong and mighty. They have a second sense for justice and truth. They instinctively know where something "stinks," that is, whenever injustice or dishonesty is at work.

9. **The Peacemaker:** They need to avoid. They are peacemakers. They accept others without prejudice, making people feel understood and accepted. However, quite often they don't have a clear sense of their own agendas.

We each have a percentage of all nine types in us, with one or two types being most predominant. I found the test to be spot on! It revealed that I'm a Helper, a Two; my main concern with all I do is to receive love and be needed. Not necessarily to be liked, but loved. A Two's default when stressed? Twos become short tempered, bossy, and very manipulative. Yikes...that is me!!!

(I strongly encourage you to take the test online. The short, free version takes about 10 minutes. Then read up on what your default responses are, and the most fun part of this is reading where you go to when you're under stress.)

The next year I asked Foster to meet with our coaching staff. We all took the Enneagram and spent a full day going over the results with Foster, learning about our comfortable defaults and where we would naturally gravitate to in times of stress. I still crack up remembering one of our coaches Randy Lane reading his assessment out loud, particularly when he got to the part that describes how he reacts when under stress. Randy laughed, threw his head back, and screamed an obscenity to the universe because it was so spot on. That is basically the same reaction everyone has when reading where they go to under stress.

The next year we asked Foster to administer the assessment test to our team. We all knew by now how beneficial it could be if the individuals on the team understood their default personality setting. There was a catch, though. Foster had never tested people as young as the members of our team; he wasn't sure if it was going to work because the brains of young adults between the ages of 18 and 22 haven't yet fully developed (MRI studies show that the prefrontal cortex of the brain, the rational part handling impulse control, personality, and other functions, continues to develop until around age 25). We wouldn't be certain if the results were accurate. Knowing that caveat we decided to give it a go. And again, the results were spot on.

In our program, once the tests are completed, we have a meeting where Foster and his wife, Cathy, debrief the girls on what the results mean. This annual team meeting is one of the most energized meetings we have all year. The girls are riveted! I love seeing how invested each of the girls is in learning more about her personality defaults and how she can choose to put space between life's stimuli and her responses. It's so empowering for the girls to realize they get to *choose* the responses they *want* to have.

Understanding your personality is not about giving you an excuse for how you behave because it is just your nature, but rather it gives you the power to choose and put yourself in successful situations. As Foster points out, "Your Enneagram shows up when you don't." You have the power to put a gap of time between something that happens and your chosen response.

Our team's volunteer assistant coach, 2011 all-around world champion and 2012 Olympic gold medalist, Jordyn Wieber shared with me how taking this test has helped her. "I'm a number Three," she said. "My default response as a Three is to go to paranoid. When I don't take a moment to think through my response, I get extremely image conscious. My insecurities come through as what will people think of me? When I take time to pause, I then start adjusting my actions/behavior to how I want to respond and how I want to be perceived by others."

The best part of the Enneagram is that it serves as one of the first tools our student-athletes have to start becoming more self-aware, especially aware of their thoughts and why they naturally gravitate toward certain familiar thoughts, which stem from their deepest insecurities. It also has proven to be an invaluable reminder for all of us to not judge each other but to take the time to pause and analyze why a teammate or coach acts the way they do.

Madison Kocian, 2016 gold medal Olympian and UCLA gymnast, told me that prior to coming to UCLA she had done a lot of work with sport psychologists. What she found interesting about the Enneagram is that while she continued to learn about herself, she said she learned even more about her coaches and her teammates. "If someone's in a weird funk or a little bit down," she said, "it helps me know how to help them."

In the nine years I've administered the Enneagram to our team there have only been two student-athletes, Lichelle Wong from Holland and Pauline Tratz from Germany, whose assessments came back inaccurate (in all of our opinions), seemingly unrelated to them. When they took the assessment in their native language their results came back much different and spot on.

Foster asserts that people who take the Enneagram are "given a language in a nonjudgmental way to look at all parts of themselves when they're emotionally healthy and when they're not." He believes the Enneagram "accelerates their maturity as an individual on this planet and as an athlete. When you've got athletes coming together from a more mature place, a less emotionally triggered place, a less highjacked place, you're going to have a better team."

When we first started doing the Enneagram we had a lot of Sevens and Eights on our team. Sevens, Enthusiasts, are like the dog in the film *Up*: "Squirrel!" Sevens are always excited to experience the next best thing even if they haven't finished the task at hand. Vanessa Zamarripa, 2010 NCAA vault champion, was a strong Seven, which is one reason she was so much fun to have on the team. However, during the years we had a lot of Sevens, I had to make sure that while I was letting our team enjoy the process, I was also paying extra attention to keeping them on task.

We recently saw an interesting trend emerge. Almost every

Olympian who has gone through our program and taken the Enneagram—Kyla Ross, Madison Kocian, and coaches Jordyn Wieber and Chris Waller—all received the same personality assessment score. They are all Achievers, all Threes. Isn't that interesting?! Out of curiosity I contacted Simone Biles, 2016 Olympic gold medalist, and Nastia Liukin, 2008 Olympic gold medalist, and asked them to take the test. Guess what? They were Threes too!

I want to stress that this isn't the predominant personality you *must* have to reach the Olympics or any level of greatness. For proof, Sam Peszek, an Olympic silver medalist, world champion, and three-time national champion for UCLA, scored highest as a Challenger, an Eight. So did Danusia Francis, Olympic alternate to the Great Britain 2012 Olympic team and 2016 NCAA balance beam champion. They are Challengers, they love competition and will fight for what's right and just 100 percent of the time.

In the last few years we've had half of our team assessed as Threes. Threes are goal oriented. Threes want a plan and want to know the plan as far in advance as possible. This drives me *crazy* as I am not naturally organized and I *love* to fly by the seat of my pants. (My second highest number is a Seven, the Enthusiast.) Coaching a team full of Threes has been great for me because it gives me a choice I can't ignore: to coach how I prefer/am naturally inclined to or to do what is best for the team. It would be easy for me to disregard their requests for order and for having a master plan because, after all, I'm the head coach; I should be able to coach per my comfort level, right? Yes, if it was all about me. And so I have acquiesced and now give our team our goals and plans weeks ahead of time—in writing! You're welcome, Threes! Yes, I'm very proud of myself; it drives me crazy, but I know it's the best thing for our team.

Going to your default is not necessarily a negative thing. Before we left for the NCAA Super Six Gymnastics Championships in 2017 (referring to the final six teams competing), my amazing friend and UCLA assistant softball coach Kirk Walker said to me, "You are what you continually do—just do what you do!" He was telling me and the team to lean on our default settings. I found it very appropriate, encouraging, and stress relieving. The truth is that while we like to imagine we are going to be different in different situations—and this can and sometimes does happen, albeit rarely—we can take comfort in knowing that we're likely to rise or fall to the level of our own default.

This is what makes everything we do every single day so vitally important. With time, what we do becomes effortless because it becomes our character. It becomes our default. It's through practice and repetition that we form habits. It's through these habits that we begin to create a lifestyle, and this cannot be gained or lost in a single instance.

No one illustrates the level of brilliance that can be achieved when your daily default is to strive for excellence better than Christine "Peng-Peng" Lee. She has shown it again and again, especially in her performances at the NCAA championships in 2017 and 2018. In 2017, on her very last routine, she mesmerized the crowd when she scored her first perfect 10 on balance beam for UCLA. Then, in 2018, she did that on bars *and* beam at the championship meet!

There has not been one day of Peng's life that she has not lived fully. I asked her parents about this and they agreed. Every moment of every day Peng has a zest for living I've never before seen. The rest of the world saw and acknowledged it on the biggest stage our collegiate environment has to offer. Peng's beam and bar routines weren't miraculous, they were merely Peng doing what she always does; a 10 has become Peng's *default*.

The important ingredient in honing your default is to hit the proverbial *refresh button* over and over and over throughout the day. Just like with a computer, when you hit your internal refresh button it trashes all of the mental junk that is getting in your way of moving toward your goal. Getting rid of the junk, which is usually negativity or things that are out of our control (but that we love to stress about), allows us to see clearly and focus on our personal path that will inch us closer to our goals. At the very least, you will wind up with clarity as to what doesn't work; then you can hit the refresh button again and try something else. For me, hitting the refresh button brings me clarity of purpose. It illuminates my ultimate goal and allows me to refocus on how to get there, instead of being stuck in the minutia of regret, negativity, or someone else's opinion.

I first thought of the *refresh button* when I started coaching balance beam and needed to come up with a simple way for the athletes to refocus. Quite often when they made a mistake on beam, they would make many more mistakes through the remainder of the routine because they were focused on the original mishap, an error they could no longer do anything about. I saw an immediate change when they bought into the refresh button concept. They would literally move on with the rest of their routine like the whole thing had been flawless. The first place this positivity and confidence showed up was in their faces. If their faces were tight I knew they hadn't embraced their refresh buttons; if they were bright and smiling I knew they had trashed any frustration and had moved on. Smiling on balance beam is one of the uncommon things I insist our athletes do because, after all, the beam is their stage. As a bonus, research shows the act of smiling releases dopamine, endorphins, and serotonin, which fight stress, relax the body, lower the heart rate and blood pressure, and act as a natural pain reliever. Just like everything in life, our default starts with our mind.

I invite you to consider this *refresh* button the next time you find yourself in a stressful situation that you have to find a way to finish, such as speaking in front of an audience. I frequently make mistakes in my speaking engagements. I've learned to immediately hit the refresh button and either clarify my mistake or simply move on as if nothing egregious has happened. I've found that 100 percent of the time when I do make a mistake and I own it, it endears me to the audience in no way a perfect presentation ever could, especially if it is something we can all laugh at.

Hitting that refresh button is a small thing that can make a big difference. As I've already mentioned, so is the pause between *reacting* to something and *responding* to it. To go back to the Enneagram for a moment, in order for the information we learn from it to have any effect, we must factor in the time it takes to pause, reflect, and choose our action. This pause is something I've paused to think about a lot lately. (Sorry, I couldn't resist.) As I mentioned earlier, when we pause to review our possible responses we not only have a better chance of not regretting our reactive decisions, but we also give ourselves a small time-out, a small breath, an exhale, a mini-moment of meditation and mindfulness.

Okay, I'm going to throw something at you that's going to seem incredibly elementary, but hear me out. One of the easiest ways we can take that pause multiple times a day is by simply saying "You're welcome." The power behind a well-meaning "You're welcome" is hugely beneficial for both parties. I noticed a few years ago that most of us are quick to give a curt "thank you" in passing, which is usually followed by an even more curt response of "sure," "no prob," or "yep." In an attempt to build greater team connectivity I began talking to our team about the importance of "You're welcome." When we take the time to acknowledge someone's "thank you" with a short pause, a look in the eye, and a sincere "You're welcome," there is a short bond of connected energy that translates to respect for each other. Considering that we could feasibly say "You're welcome" over a hundred times a day, imagine how that kindness would translate to your own inner calm, peacefulness, and feeling of goodwill. Priceless moments of calm captured in kindness toward another...what seems elementary—and so very small—is actually strengthening the fibers of your relationship with that person.

Chapter Eight

It All Matters

"What you wear is how you present yourself to the world, especially today, when human contacts are so quick. Fashion is instant language."

—Miuccia Prada

Early on in my head coaching career I was in the athletic department when I ran into our athletic director who was with a major donor. I was mortified because I was wearing baggy sweatpants and a sweatshirt, didn't have any makeup on, and my hair was thrown up in the ubiquitous high sloppy ponytail of a female athlete. This was *not* how I would have chosen to represent UCLA and our program had I been given notice that I'd be meeting my boss and a donor. I wanted to say, "Could you excuse me while I go freshen up a bit, and could I meet you all over again in about 15 minutes?"

The proverb "You never get a second chance to make a first impression" is absolutely true. It isn't about how I might be perceived or judged by someone else, because that is out of my control. The important part is that I need to accept that an opinion will be formulated about me from the *moment* I meet someone else. In one small instant, someone will be deciding who they think I am. So I need to take control over how I act and look in order to help shape that opinion—that is, if I care. Sometimes I don't. Most of the time I do.

Let's face it, we all judge other people. Most of us like to think that we don't. However, the ability to observe without judging takes deliberate intention and awareness, at least for me. The ability to look at someone and *not* formulate a notion of what they're like as a person is a skill that I need to exercise with constant repetition to strengthen like a muscle.

At that moment with the athletic director and the donor, my mind went back to my youth and the Sacramento ballet studio where I grew up dancing. Our ballet teacher was Miss Ingrid Carriker. She was simply lovely. I remember being in my early teens when it hit me how nice it was that Miss Ingrid showed up every day beautifully coifed and dressed. She obviously took great care with her leotard and matching ballet skirt. Her hair and makeup were always nicely done and even though she smoked, she always had breath mints.

The subliminal message that Miss Ingrid gave all of us young dancers was that we were important, and the class we were about to take was important because she had taken the time to look her best for the class. This is something I've instilled in our athletes. We train at 7:45 in the morning, which means most of them are in the training room by 6:30 a.m. getting treatment. Regardless of what time they need to be on campus, I ask them to show up looking presentable and not like they just rolled out of bed. Not only do they represent UCLA gymnastics to everyone they see each morning, but we all know how much better we feel when we like how we look.

Miss Ingrid was the epitome of a polished lovely lady. "Polished lovely lady" is a description I'd like to embody. Sloppy sweats and zero attention to face and hair don't exactly scream that. So, ever since that day, I always take a few extra minutes the night before to plan my attire for the next day. Then I make sure to get up in time to do my hair and makeup before I head out the door. It's not about having an amazing wardrobe. It's about taking the time and care to match your appearance with how you want to be perceived.

As I've said, I don't get to decide how others judge me. I can, however, influence their impression of me from the moment I walk into a room. My presentation to the world is a choice and speaks volumes long before I even open my mouth. In a world where we're judged on our appearance, whether it's for a job interview, a date, or unexpectedly bumping into a major financial donor, our appearance matters.

Perception is reality, including how you perceive yourself. When I take the time and care to present myself in the manner that I want to, I literally stand taller and more confidently, and that impression is exactly what I want to convey in life and as the leader for the UCLA gymnastics program.

What you say to yourself can also have an impact on your presentation and performance. For example, you can wear an amazing outfit to a meeting, but if you enter the room rehearsing the wrong internal dialogue it can derail all of your outward preparation. When I have found myself in this situation I have worked to find the right internal "cue."

For example, in the past, if I was heading into a meeting with one of our coaches and I knew we were going to discuss a touchy subject, I would coach myself up with an internal cue that goes like this: "I know I've thought this through, and I believe I'm right, so I can't be afraid to stand up for what I believe is best for the team." The problem is that cue would immediately put me on the defensive, which is obviously not a good place to start a conversation, especially a sensitive one. That meant it was time to hit the refresh button. I had to get the negativity and my personal agenda out of the way and reset the cue to "*listen.*" It's one small word with a ton of meaning. In order to execute this new cue I understood that I needed to silence my brain when the other person was talking. This new cue immediately established a more collaborative starting place for the conversation. It was "Let's figure out what's best for the team" versus a noncollaborative "I'm going to explain to you why I'm right." The entry point in a conversation, established by a simple internal cue, can make a big difference in the outcome. In fact, if I am ever at a loss for a cue, my default is always "Listen," or actually, "Shut up and listen."

As a coach, in order to help athletes achieve the results they want, I help them come up with cues to say before each skill that emphasizes some finer points. Take balance beam, for example. Some athletes have a technical cue they say to themselves, such as "push through my legs" or "jump," before they do their flipping series. Other athletes have emotional cues, such as "patience" or "aggressive," that they say in their heads before they execute the skill.

Kristina Comforte was an intensely fierce competitor who helped us win our sixth championship in 2010. Her cue was a little different. I noticed that whenever she was ready and on her game, she would flare her nostrils with intensity. So during one of her first home meets I told her, "Flare your nostrils on the beam and I'll know you're good to go."

As a coach, it is vitally important to communicate with the athletes to make sure a cue is resonating with them in a way that will help produce positive results. One of my most humbling memories of this is working with 2001–2004 UCLA gymnast Yvonne Tousek on beam. She was super consistent but always had a slight knee bend in her back handspring and layout step out. I tried a ton of different cues, including "Jump through your legs," "Split later," "Push through your feet," "Aggressive set," and more. Finally, at one meet she executed the skill perfectly.

When I asked her what she told herself before executing the skill she responded, "I simply said, 'Strong Legs.'" Even though the cues I had given her were meant to accomplish the same thing, nothing resonated with her until she came up with her *own* cue. What felt right for me didn't resonate with her. I would have never thought to tell her those exact two little words. That was a great life lesson for me.

When you find a cue that works it can last a lifetime. Great life cues can calibrate your inner calm, focus, and purpose. Kim Hamilton was a spectacular UCLA gymnast who won three consecutive NCAA floor exercise titles. Roughly 30 years ago, when Kim was a freshman, she and I came up with her cue: "Go have fun!"

Miss Val didn't coach me on tumbling, she didn't tell me how to stick my landings or do any of those things, but there is one thing she did tell me starting my freshman year. "Go have fun." The first time she said this to me was at nationals in Utah, when I was getting ready to compete in the floor finals. The competition was pretty stiff and I was only a freshman. One of our coaches told me how to execute my tumbling passes. And then Miss Val saunters over and with a big smile says, "Kimmy, go have fun." With that I was reminded of the fun I would have performing as opposed to how tight the competition was. I felt invincible. I won floor nationals that year and then the two consecutive years after that. Every time I approached the floor she would come to me and say those words and each time they had the same effect on me. "Kimmy, go have fun." Which I translated as be who you are, enjoy the gift you've been given, trust in your preparation, and allow the whole world to see it.

Much more recently, Kim was a guest speaker at a large event, and was feeling just a bit nervous. The photographer for the event had read Kim's book, *Unfavorable Odds*, in which she mentions the cue. As she was about to go onstage the photographer said, "Hey Kim, just have fun."

"Immediately I see Miss Val's face and those big ol' eyes telling me to have fun. It worked. It brought me back and I probably had the most fun speaking at that event than at any event I have done."

In 2003, I, then newly appointed assistant coach Chris Waller, and the entire UCLA women's gymnastics team experienced the true power of cues. We were about to head off to our first real meet of the season at the University of Utah—an intimidating proposition. It's almost impossible to exaggerate how dominant the Utes women's gymnastics program was from the late 70s to the mid-90s.

The greatest streaks in sports are typically talked about in games or even years. The longest home winning streak in NCAA gymnastics history didn't last years, though; it lasted decades, and it belongs to Greg Marsden's women's gymnastics program. From February of 1979 to January of 2003, every team that entered Jon M. Huntsman Center in Utah left with a loss on their record. Then the Bruins arrived and we broke their 170–home meet win streak—at least that's what I'm told because I wasn't there.

I had a meeting on campus when my neck suddenly went into spasms. I couldn't move it. I made my way to our athletic training room, where I was advised not to travel. It was Chris's first official collegiate meet and he was going to have to travel into the most dominant arena in the country as the acting head coach!

"I was nervous as hell," Chris later shared. Once the team got to the airport, Chris called and asked me 1,000 questions. But some of the most important information I gave him was all the individual mental cues for each athlete on balance beam, the event for which I was the sole coach. I told Chris what to say to each gymnast and *how* to say it per each personality. I found out later that he quickly scribbled everything down on three-by-five-inch index cards.

I remember being on the phone during the meet with Liza David, our sports information director, who gave me the play-by-play. On the first event, uneven bars, two UCLA gymnasts fell. I was going crazy just lying on my couch at home; I felt totally helpless to assist our team in any way and was thinking, "Poor Chris. Poor team. Starting off the meet with two falls … this is going to be a *long* night."

The balance beam was next. Chris later said he literally read from the index cards, and also got some help from the other gymnasts. Jamie Dantzscher told a reporter after the meet that she learned what I would say to her teammates and repeated the phrases and cues to help Chris out.

Chris remembers bits of the instructions he read: "For Kristen Parker, put your hand on her shoulder, look her in the eye, and tell her she's performing for an audience of One. She has a strong faith and getting her to perform for God alone will calm her down." "For Doni Thompson, just remind her how amazing she is and tell her to 'just do you,' while giving her the good ol' fist bump." "For Yvonne Tousek, put your hands on her shoulders and tell her to trust her training."

The team crushed beam. They propelled themselves forward into the final two events with an exuberance and confidence that allowed them to do something no one else had done since the 1970s—beat the Utes in their home gym.

It proved to be an "aha" coaching experience for Chris. He recalls that it made him realize that to be successful he had to coach way more than just the skills. As he explains, "You're coaching an emotional human being, that means you have to help get them in the right state of mind and not just remind them of their technical cues. The words matter; how you say the words matters; whether or not you touch their shoulder or their elbow matters. It *all* matters. I paid attention to those emotional details and it paid off."

Take time to appreciate the value of seemingly small things and consider developing a mental cue or two to help yourself through stressful times. Actually don't just consider it, do it. There is only positivity that will come from establishing a cue that is simple, resonates, and will help you hit the refresh button to be your best you.

Chapter Nine

Blooming in the Desert

"Those destined for greatness must first walk alone in the desert."
—Winston Churchill

I don't want my positive outlook on life to make you think of me as an out-of-touch Pollyanna. I realize that life can be unfair, but our response to our circumstances is still a choice—especially when you find yourself in an "emotional desert."

I'll never forget when Jeanette Antolin, one of the women who appeared on *60 Minutes*, was halfway through her sophomore year at UCLA. One day, she was just lying on her back in the gym when she should have been training with the rest of the team. I went up to her and asked, "What's up?"

She looked at me and said, "Miss Val, I don't ever want anyone to tell me what to do *ever* again."

I chuckled a bit and replied, "Well honey, then I think you need to go find a deserted island to live on because that's just not how life works."

In the days and weeks that followed Jeanette broke a few more team rules and she also skipped some of her classes. As a result she was eventually removed from the team, and that meant she also lost her scholarship to UCLA.

I'll never forget her stoic behavior when I told her this painful news. I had thought, based on the attitude and behavior that had gotten her to this point, she would be glad that she didn't have to abide by the rules of our program anymore. I was wrong. Reality hit and her tears started. Jeanette sobbed in my office and followed me to the gym, clutching my arm, continuing to sob, and pleading with me to change my mind. It was at this point everything became so clear to me. Jeanette was in the "desert."

I looked at her and gleefully said, "Jeanette, this is going to be the best year of your life."

This is *not* at all what she expected my reaction to be. I cannot tell you how many athletes I've annoyed over the years as they go through a similar experience. They sit in my office distraught over a boulder that life has thrown in their path and by the poor choices they made that got them dismissed from the team. As they sit there downtrodden, tears streaming, totally deflated, I look into their sad eyes with a twinkle of excitement and say, "This is going to be *amazing*! You're in the desert—and it's going to be sooo good!" I get the same bewildered look from each and every one of them.

Jeanette was a USAG national team member and in her freshman season with us she was amazing, helping us win another national championship. We had been expecting big things from Jeanette heading into her sophomore season, but taking a walk in the proverbial desert was what was going to be best for *her*. I had come to learn that the desert is a magical place where transformation happens. This transformation is possible because the desert is an isolating place where all outside noise and distractions have been silenced. All comforts and crutches are absent in the desert, and your focus is on personal survival. In the desert your potential gets challenged; you discover how tough and resilient you are. In the desert you become creative and driven. You take action and ownership of your situation. You learn to rely on and trust yourself, and eventually the magic happens and you find that you actually like yourself.

Everyone ends up in the desert at least once, and probably multiple times, in their life. We all need to be able to recognize when we are in the desert and to embrace it; our next choices will either lead us one step closer to changing and eventually emerging or result in us digging deeper into the depressed misery of desert life.

Jeanette did not want to hear about the journey she was about to embark on and definitely didn't understand it—I'm also fairly certain I was not one of her favorite people at that moment. But, I knew with 100 percent certainty that this was going to be the best year of her life.

With no one to bail her out and pay for all of her expenses, schooling, rent, and so on, Jeanette got student loans and immediately did what was needed to become a certified athletic perfor-mance trainer. She worked with clients in the early morning, went to her classes at UCLA, and worked some more at night.

About six months later, a few of the girls on the team came to my office and said they wanted me to reconsider letting Jeanette back on the team. They all confirmed she had *really* changed. She was moti-vated, excited about life, and happy. She'd even cut up her fake ID. Now *that* was serious. She had also been going into the open gym at night to continue her gymnastics training on her own. I told the girls to tell Jeanette I'd stop by the open gym sometime soon.

It felt like my eyes were bulging right out of my face when I saw her! She was unbelievably physically fit and blasted a sky-high vault. "Uhhhhhhhh, okay...I'll meet with her," I decided.

It was vital that I decipher if Jeanette had really changed or if she was just acting the way she thought she needed to in order to get back on the team. If the latter were the case, she'd just end up back in the desert.

It turned out that Jeanette had been doing gymnastics for her-self, not so she could return to the team. In fact, she confessed she didn't think she would be returning to the UCLA gymnastics team. She had truly changed. Jeanette was so proud of her recent accom-plishments and that she could fully lean on and trust herself. Jeanette joined our team midseason that year—without a scholarship—and helped our team win an NCAA championship. She became a valu-able leader for the remainder of her time in our program.

"I was really able to see how strong of a person I was and that I could trust myself again," Jeanette has said about being in the desert. "And really, I learned that I could get through anything because, honestly, that was the hardest thing I had ever gone through in my life."

She has said that this desert experience while at UCLA helped her to be able to come forward and testify about the US gymnastics abuse case. "I can look back at situations like the one with Miss Val and UCLA and it's like, well I got through that. So, I know I'm strong enough and I can get through this. Everyone has ups and downs in their life. It's how you choose to handle them that will determine the life you live."

My husband tells me all the time, "My Love, all the flowers in the garden don't bloom at the same time." As long as they keep on blooming, no matter how painfully slow it feels, then I'll allow them to be a part of the team with the hope that at some point they'll have their aha moment.

I've written about the desert concept on my website (Official MissVal.com) and have been flooded with responses from people telling me about their own desert experiences. It's a testament to the fact we *all* visit the desert.

Unfortunately, some people choose to dwell in the desert. They say they can't progress because they are in quicksand; but if they were to pause and really look at their circumstances, they'd realize they were being stubborn and burying their toes into the sand. For these kinds of people, it is easier to lament about their "lot in life" than realize that they have a choice whether or not to stay in the desert.

I feel so badly for people who choose to stay in the desert instead of summoning up the discipline and determination to do what it takes to get out. I don't understand how being a desert dweller is more satisfying than expending the necessary energy to get out into the world of the thriving.

The first thing I do when I find myself in the desert is seek out a close friend who will be brutally honest with me without being judgmental. Having them put a proverbial mirror in front of my face is usually all I need to start making decisions that will allow me to guide myself out of the desert.

My most intense desert experience happened when I was 48 years old and going through a midlife crisis. It also happened to coincide with my 10-year wedding anniversary. I was bored. I was moody. I was apathetic. I was sad. I didn't give a hoot about anything, let alone my marriage. In trying to figure out what was really wrong, I had a very convenient person on whom to place blame, Bobby. He's so extremely easygoing, I could get away with being a total brat. So I placed the blame on him; *he* was the problem, *he* wasn't making my life exciting.

I spewed all of this out to one of my dearest friends, Paul Chiames. After he chuckled and took a deep breath, Paul said, "From how I see it, Bobby hasn't changed, you have. He's still the same man you married. So what's different?"

I was struck silent. And then came clarity. Why was I waiting for Bobby to make my life exciting? I had everything in my power to have an amazing life *especially* with Bobby. Not only is he always kind, loving, considerate, respectful, complimentary, extremely self-sufficient, capable—yes he is *all that all the time*—but he always cracks me up, and, this is where some of my married girlfriends get really jealous, he has absolutely no problem with me *doing my thing*. Whether it's going out with friends, going to the theatre, going out recruiting for four to six weeks at a time, going to San Diego to choreograph for a month in the spring…he has *never ever ever* made me feel guilty for living a full life and has always encouraged me to pursue my dreams.

So with that realization, my midlife crisis quickly melted away, and I started taking charge of my life and happiness again.

The next time you find yourself in the desert, just remember it will be painful, but it truly is a gift. I don't look forward to my next stint in the desert, but I don't fear it either. I know that when that time does come I will be fully equipped to get through it and come out a better version of myself. Every time I make my way out of the desert, I am wiser, more humble, more compassionate, and more determined to live my life to the fullest.

It bears repeating that whether it's your internal thoughts or your external circumstances that are less than ideal, you still have the choice either to be miserable or choose to embrace your situation. In fact, the military has a saying for it: "Embrace the suck." I love this term—it even feels good to say it.

I've done it. Back in 1985, three years after I had quit dancing, I decided I missed it and wanted to take a dance class. Whatever the word for "beyond sucked" is, that was me. I couldn't believe how much my muscle strength and technique had deteriorated. I was literally no more than five minutes into the class and my legs wouldn't stop shaking. Dance class was sooo not fun. I was miserable; consequently, I didn't dance for many years except to choreograph, and even then I demonstrated as little as possible because my dancing felt nothing like it used to. It simply wasn't fun anymore because I didn't have the skill, technique, and strength that I used to have. The full weight of this hit me when I was choreographing a floor routine and was trying to demonstrate an intricate leap and turn down to the floor where I was to swirl around and rebound right back up to my feet—uhhhhh, come on body...get off the floor! It literally took me a full eight counts to lift my sorry butt off the floor because I had been so inactive for so long. It was time for a change!

I decided to embrace the suck. I realized how much I missed moving to music. I missed learning choreography. I missed the hardwood floor and hearing the instructor count us in with, "Ahhh 5, 6, 7, 8." And most of all, I missed getting lost in the spirit of dance.

Once I realized all of this, I also realized how my ego was preventing me from enjoying something my soul craved. I remember looking around in the next dance class I decided to take; I realized that the most inspiring dancer in the class was a very overweight woman in tights and a leotard. She was reveling in her ability to move and was literally lost in the spirit of dance—something I'd been missing for a long, long time. I also realized looking around that dance class that no one was looking at me. "Get over yourself, Valorie. Nobody cares if you're great or you suck, so just enjoy the movement."

Perception isn't just about how someone perceives you, it's also about how you perceive and approach the world. A while back I was having a nice little conversation with my coauthor, Coop. He had just gotten through playing golf, so I asked him how it went.

"Actually I sucked, but it was a great day. The weather was amazing, the golf course was beautiful, I was with friends, and I decided I was going to enjoy my terrible play," Coop told me. "I had a talk with myself and said, 'I love to golf. But I don't have the time right now to work on my golf game—and I know I need to consistently play to get better. So I can either get upset because I suck—and I *hate* not striving for greatness in everything I do—or I can give myself permission to suck knowing I'm not putting in the time to be great so I should enjoy every other aspect of the experience.'"

Embracing the suck is a *choice*. Embracing the suck means you are embracing your humility. Embracing the suck is a level of self-awareness where you know your best is not what is going to stand out at this particular moment in time. In fact, the only thing that will stand out is the great attitude you exude while you suck. When you embrace the suck you are giving yourself permission to take more risks and to be more vulnerable and adventurous. Here's to embracing the suck. Allow yourself to enjoy doing something simply because you think it's fun and it makes your heart sing.

Chapter Ten

Helping Athletes Find Their Joy

"The joy of learning is as indispensable in study as breathing is in running."

—Simone Weil

It's difficult to give ourselves permission to feel joy in doing something that, from a technical point of view, we may not be very good at—dancing, playing golf, whatever our inner voice is drawing us toward. But can you imagine being not just good, but *great* at something and not being able to find or feel the joy in *that* pursuit? I've never understood why anyone, particularly a coach, would want to take the joy out of learning! Sucking at something is part of the learning process. I feel so badly for our youth who aren't encouraged to embrace the suck while working to learn a skill. The need to always be "perfect" stifles growth, creates unwarranted stress, and totally takes the fun out of the challenge of learning.

Over the three-plus decades of my UCLA career I have had innumerable encounters with gymnasts as well as parents and coaches who had been pushed to silence their voices and their spirits. Helping our student-athletes find their voices is an imperative part of my job. It's something that most of them haven't learned because of the strict gym environments they've grown up in. I use every opportunity to get them to learn to feel comfortable voicing their opinions and thoughts, regardless of whether or not they feel they will be well received. I especially like it when they find the guts to come back at me and question my decisions. I tell them *all* the time, you can say anything to anyone as long as you are being *honest* and *respectful*. This has offered a great training ground for them to learn the fine art of diplomacy.

The first rule of thumb is don't question my decisions in front of other team members unless it's a meeting in my office with only people who are necessary to the conversation. And second, don't challenge or embarrass me in front of others and I promise to do the same for you. I've definitely crossed this line in my career when I thought it would be beneficial to other team members to hear and witness my frustration. In hindsight, that was a mistake. The line between holding an athlete accountable and belittling them is one that should be held sacred for the sake of the athlete's well-being, the coach–athlete relationship, and the overarching health and culture of the program.

Let me share just a few of my many early encounters with tre-

At the ballet barre, 1976. I was 16 years old. (Author Collection)

Amos, Greece, 1964. Yes, that's me at 4 years old with our donkey Maria. (Author Collection)

Hanging out with Jim Stephenson before a competition circa 1976. (Author Collection)

My beautiful mom, 1978. Everyone who knew my mom absolutely adored her. She was pure Love. (Author Collection)

My last performance before I retired and came to UCLA. (Author Collection)

Oh my ... my first year at UCLA, 1982. *Back row, left to right:* Donna Kemp, Deanne Koulos, and Michelle Ehrlich. *Second row, left to right:* Scott Bull, SueEllen League, Anne Kitabayashi, Karen Cogan, and Gigi Ambandos. *Front row, left to right:* me, Kim Berry, Janet Ferrari, Tracy Curtis, Kris Montera, Rhonda Schwandt, and Jerry Tomlinson. (Photo courtesy of UCLA Athletics)

Gotta love the 80s. In our training gym, 1987. Big Hair, lots of makeup and check out the nails! (Author Collection)

My dad and my brother Steven at his wedding, 1989. Our mom had passed in 1985. (Author Collection)

Marrying the man of my dreams in our Big Fat Greek Wedding, 1998, in Sacramento, California. (Author Collection)

With the great Coach John Wooden, circa 2004. Coach died in 2010, 4 months shy of 100 years old. (Author Collection)

Coach Wooden and me in his home for our interview with *UCLA Magazine*, 2006. (Photo by Gregg Segal)

The coaching staff visits the White House after winning the 2010 NCAA Championship: P.J. Irvin, me, Chris Waller, and Jim Foody. (Author Collection)

Chillin' with my husband in Westwood. He's simply the best! (Author Collection)

Just hanging out with our favorite numbers, enjoying warmups before a competition. (Author Collection)

On set for *Full Out*, the movie about the life of UCLA gymnast Ariana Berlin. *Left to right:* me, Ariana, Ana Golja (who plays Ariana), Sean Cisterna (the film's director), and the brilliant Jennifer Beals (who plays Miss Val). (Author Collection)

Choreographing a gymnastic floor routine, 2014. (Photo by Christy Linder)

Wow—if you could harness the competitive spirit in these three, bottle it up, and sell it ... it would ignite the galaxy. The blondes, from left to right: Alicia Sacramone, Sam Peszek, and Kristina Comforte. (Author Collection)

Jordyn Wieber in my office, sitting on Coach Wooden's sofa and preparing for her first day as an assistant coach at UCLA, September 26, 2016. (Author Collection)

Sadiqua Bynum with her life-changing mohawk. (Photo by Christy Linder)

When in L.A. ... I love the fact that there's a guy in hot pink shorts stretching with our team. Oh wait, that's Olympic medalist Danell Leyva. (Author Collection)

Me with Christian Sanchez, one of the many SeaWorld performers we've groomed who later went on to perform in Le Reve and Cirque du Soleil. Hugging it out after a performance of Cirque du Soleil's *Avatar*. (Author Collection)

Madison Kocian and me just hanging out, holding hands, 2018. There's something magical about holding someone's hand. (Author Collection)

The two shows I've been working on at SeaWorld. Check out the flying Dolphin in the bottom venue. And the performer on the laser platform at the far left is Peng-Peng Lee. (Author Collection)

Enjoying the spirit of Dance in a dance camp. (Photo by Stephanie Schmidt Othersen)

The red carpet for the *Jump Jive and Thrive* TV special honoring cancer survivors: Jordyn Wieber, Brandy Johnson, Sam Peszek, Betty Okino, and me. This was a few months before the #MeToo movement hit the mainstream. Ironically, the song they performed to in this show was "Me Too," by Meghan Trainor. (Photo by Deanna Hong)

Bobby Field is inducted into the UCLA Athletic Hall of Fame, October 2017. We became the only married couple inducted into the Hall. Isn't he adorable! (Author Collection)

Me with my second mom, Nan Wooden, Coach Wooden's daughter. (Author Collection)

Our team with two of our UCLA Greats: NCAA Champions Heidi Moneymaker (*middle*) and Jeanette Antolin and her son Mekhi. (Author Collection)

How I keep track of choreography when I'm at home working on more than one piece. The ponytail tells me which way the athlete should be facing. This was Kyla's 2018 routine. (Author Collection)

Spontaneous jubilation: Katelyn Ohashi being raised by her teammates after receiving a 10.0 on floor at our Teal Meet, 2018. (Author Collection)

Celebrating strong athletes coming together for change in our sport, #TogetherWeRise. This Teal Meet in 2018, UCLA vs. Oklahoma, was the most important gymnastics event in our history. *Left to right:* Maggie Nichols, Jamie Dantzscher, Jeanette Antolin, Mattie Larson, and Jordyn Wieber. (Author Collection)

Peng-Peng Lee celebrating with our team at the 2018 NCAA Championships, one of the most epic comebacks in all sport! (Author Collection)

The 2018 NCAA coaching staff after we won the Championship: Jordyn Wieber, Randy Lane, me, Hallie Mossett, and Chris Waller. (Author Collection)

The 1997 NCAA Championship Team. *Back row, left to right:* Susie Erickson, Carmen Tausend, Lena Degteva, Deborah Mink, Amy Smith, and Lisa Hiley. *Second row, left to right:* Andrea Fong and Heidi Moneymaker. *Front row, left to right:* Stella Umeh, Luisa Portacarrero, Leah Homma, and Kiralee Hayashi. (Photo courtesy of UCLA Athletics)

The 2000 NCAA Championship Team. *Back row, left to right:* Carly Raab, Stephanie Johnson, Doni Thompson, Valerie Velasco, Onnie Willis, Malia Jones, and Alison Stoner. *Front row, left to right:* Heidi Moneymaker, Amy Young, Kristin Parker, Lena Degteva, Mohini Bhardwaj, and Lindsey Dong. (Photo courtesy of UCLA Athletics)

The 2001 NCAA Championship Team. *Back row, left to right:* Mohini Bhardwaj, Malia Jones, Stephanie Johnson, Jamie Dantzscher, Jamie Williams, Doni Thompson, Kristin Parker, Carly Raab, and Valerie Velasco. *Front row, left to right:* Lindsey Dong, Onnie Willis, Jeanette Antolin, Yvonne Tousek, and Kristen Maloney. (Photo courtesy of UCLA Athletics)

The 2003 NCAA Championship Team. *Back row, left to right:* Yvonne Tousek, Alyssa Beckerman, Jamie Williams, Carly Raab, Onnie Willis, Doni Thompson, Holly Murdock, and Trishna Patel. *Second row, left to right:* Malia Jones, Kristin Parker, Jamie Dantzscher, Kristen Maloney, and Christy Erickson. *Front row, left to right:* Kate Richardson, Christy Tedmon, and Jeanette Antolin. (Photo courtesy of UCLA Athletics)

The 2004 NCAA Championship Team. *Back row, left to right:* Aimee Walker, Ashley Peckett, Holly Murdock, Ashley Martin, and Michelle Selesky. *Second row, left to right:* Jamie Williams, Christy Tedmon, Lori Winn, Kisha Auld, Jennifer Sutton, Kate Richardson, and Courtney Walker. *Front row, left to right:* Trishna Patel, Yvonne Tousek, Kristen Maloney, Jamie Dantzscher, Jeanette Antolin, and Christy Erickson. (Photo courtesy of UCLA Athletics)

The 2010 NCAA Championship Team. *Back row, left to right:* Tauny Frattone, Tiffany Hyland, Dani Greig, and Courtney Shannon. *Second row, left to right:* Allison Taylor, Vanessa Zamarripa, Lichelle Wong, Marci Bernholz, Brittani McCullough, Kaelie Baer, and Aisha Gerber. *Front row, left to right:* Talia Kushynski, Monique DeLaTorre, Anna Li, Elyse Hopfner-Hibbs, Niki Tom, Mizuki Sato, and Alyssa Pritchett. (Photo courtesy of UCLA Athletics)

The 2018 NCAA Championship Team. *Back row, left to right:* Grace Glenn, Felicia Hano, Katelyn Ohashi, Kyla Ross, Nia Dennis, Pauline Tratz, Matteah Brow, Gracie Kramer, Karli Dugas, Savannah Kooyman, Melissa Metcalf, Rechelle Dennis, and Madison Kocian. *Front row, left to right:* Brielle Nguyen, JaNay Honest, Sonya Meraz, Peng-Peng Lee, Pua Hall, and Anna Glenn. (Photo courtesy of UCLA Athletics)

mendous athletes who, in their previous training experiences, had their voices silenced through ridicule and fear.

Rhonda Faehn, former senior vice president for USAG, was a UCLA student-athlete from 1989 to 1992. She witnessed my transition from assistant to head coach her sophomore year. She was there for my struggles and has seen my evolution as both a coach and person. After she injury-retired during her senior year in 1992, Rhonda worked alongside me as a student assistant coach for two years.

Rhonda remembers how difficult the transition was when she first moved from the national team where she didn't have a voice to UCLA where she was *expected* to have a voice. When Rhonda first arrived, I told her she could have tremendous success in gymnastics *and* have fun. She told me that at the time she was thinking, "Are you crazy? What are you talking about? Gymnastics is serious." I had to demonstrate to Rhonda, over time, what having joy in the sport *and* the process looked like.

Rhonda recently told me how Martha Karolyi once gave a correction to which she, Rhonda, offered a confirming response, "Okay." Martha then replied, "Don't say 'okay,' because you're the one making the mistake." Baffled, Rhonda turned to her teammate and asked, "What do I do?" The only solution the two could come up with was to just stand there and not say anything.

This became a problem early on during her gymnastics career at UCLA, before I knew what she had gone through with Martha. I would give Rhonda a correction and she wouldn't say a thing. I remember thinking, "The least she could do is acknowledge the correction and say okay."

Just as I had worked to find my voice in coaching, Rhonda went on and did the same. In 2013 Rhonda led the University of Florida women's gymnastics team to their first national championship. At the time she became just the fifth gymnastics coach to lead her team to a national championship, and the first new coach to join those ranks after I had become the fourth 16 years earlier.

Kim Hamilton who in addition to her floor championships also won the vault title in 1989. Kim has said that her freshman year at UCLA was the *first* time she was able to have fun doing gymnastics. Imagine that! During her elite career Kim would get punished and told to do push-ups simply for *smiling* because her coaches assumed she was playing around and not taking it seriously.

Jamie Dantzscher, as previously mentioned, is truly one of the all-time gymnastics greats. You can imagine my surprise when during the second meet of her freshman year Jamie told me, "I don't want to do this anymore." Jamie always got nervous competing. She later told me that when she was an elite gymnast her coaches regularly yelled at her; of course, that only made her *more* nervous. Jamie recalled getting in trouble one time for trying to speak up to her coach. She was told she was being disrespectful. "I felt like I couldn't say anything anymore," she told me. "I remember one time getting a correction and I said, 'I know,' because I felt it, I felt her correction, and I was like, 'I know I can feel it.'" Her coach replied, "Don't say, 'I know,' that's so disrespectful."

Jamie continued, "At the Ranch, we were stripped of any individuality. We were like little robots. We all had to wear our hair a
certain way, we had to stand a certain way, we couldn't speak; you
didn't even want to look in a different direction." Her spirit had
been extinguished through ridicule and fear.

When Jamie told me *during a meet* that she didn't want to compete anymore, I told her, "Jamie, you don't *have* to do this." I then
pointed to a group of little girls in the stands who were holding signs
with her name on them. I said, "Do you think they care how many
times you fall or mess up? They came here to cheer you on because
they fell in love with *you*, the ups, the downs, the victories, and the
non-victories. So, if you can't do it for yourself today, choose to do it
for those young girls who are so excited to see you perform." Jamie
told me that because I wasn't yelling at her and was calm she chose
to really *listen* and, therefore, what I was saying began to resonate.
She believed that it would be okay to mess up and that she could
just be herself and do gymnastics. *Success is peace of mind in knowing
you've done your best.*

Finding her voice was a process. I remember during one practice
Jamie came up to me and asked, "What's our assignment?" I replied,
"What do you think you should do today?" Jamie just stared back
at me. Later she told me how she thought it was some perverse test.
She couldn't believe this wasn't a trick and that I would actually ask
her for her opinion. I wanted her input because she had been doing
gymnastics for 15 years, whereas I had only been coaching her for

two months. Obviously she knew what she needed to be confident in competition better than I did.

I said to her, "You need to figure out what you need to do to be ready for our meet this weekend." She told me, "In my mind I'm thinking she's f*#&ing joking right now."

I then said, "Seriously, if you think it's zero and you can hit a great routine in the competition this weekend, that's fine with me. Go do cardio, go to the next event, or go study." Jamie continued to be wary and admitted to me that she was a bit scared and it took a long time for her to trust me and realize she actually did have a choice, which wouldn't come out until she found her voice.

In reflecting on coming forward over a decade later to speak about being abused, Jamie has said, "I think for so long I was silenced, I wasn't allowed to talk. Had I not gone to UCLA and been with Miss Val, I don't think I would have had the tools or the confidence to deal with the abuse issue. I don't know if I would have been strong enough to speak up."

My experience with encouraging Jamie to figure out what she needed to do to be prepared for a meet was by no means unique. I remember when Kristen Maloney and Yvonne Tousek were both freshmen on our team. Kristen was a three-time US national champion and 2000 Olympian and Yvonne was a three-time world champion competitor and a two-time Olympian. They came to me in the middle of the competition season and asked what the balance beam assignment was. I almost went ahead and told them but then I thought, "Hold on. Why are these two superstar 20-year-old gymnasts asking me, someone who's only coached them for five months, what they should do on beam to prepare?"

Instead, I asked them, "What do you think you need to do to be prepared?" They were flabbergasted, just as Jamie had been. Kristen then replied, "Miss Val, just tell us what to do." I guess they had never been asked that and so I dug my heels in deeper and refused to tell them what to do. I remember laughing and saying, "I absolutely am not going to tell you what to do. You are two of the best gymnasts in the world. If you don't know what you need to do to get prepared for a meet in three days then you need to figure out how to figure it out."

They were not happy with me. I couldn't believe they didn't relish the opportunity to do whatever they wanted on beam that day and instead were begging me for the assignment.

Katelyn Ohashi, a current UCLA Bruin, was considered one of the greatest gymnasts in the world when she was in her early teens. But by the time she was 15, she felt burnt out and decided not to train for the 2016 Olympic Games in Rio. Instead, in the fall of 2016, Katelyn came to UCLA. Later that year, in a midseason team meeting, Dr. Bill Parham, our sport psychologist, was explaining how we all have an "anchor" inside of us that is holding us back from reaching our full potential. "Some anchors are mightier than others," he said. Dr. P (as he's affectionately known) then went around the room and asked each athlete to share what they thought was holding them down. When he got to Katelyn she unabashedly said, "I just don't want to be great again." *What?!*

When Katelyn had first arrived at UCLA she had fully embraced her newfound "freedom" from the regimented training she had experienced since she was 12 years old, the normal training regimen of an elite young gymnast hoping to make an Olympic team. As a byproduct, Katelyn had quite a bit of weight gain on her 4 foot 10 inch body. And since our sport is based on physics, her new body composition took its toll on her gymnastics ability. In club gymnastics, pre-college, a gymnast normally trains six days a week for anywhere from four to eight hours a day. During the collegiate competition season, they train at most three times a week for about three hours a day. The best teams we've had have actually trained the least. They understood that they had spent the past 10 or so years putting in the numbers. The gymnast who makes it to college has banked the necessary 10,000 repetitions of a skill—a reference to the 10,000 hour rule first observed by economist Herbert Simon and psychologist William Chase, and later popularized by author Malcom Gladwell—to be able to perform it anytime, anywhere, under any circumstances.

When a gymnast comes to college the whole dynamic of the sport she has known all her life changes. In club gymnastics, the better you get the less you compete. Good gymnasts who reach Junior Olympic Levels 9 and 10 status will compete about eight times a year. Elite athletes who make the US national team and represent their country internationally compete a maximum of three to five times per year. Granted they "compete" in monthly verifications at the national team training center, but that is a closed environment;

the only people there are the national team coaching staff, the athletes, and their personal coaches.

In college, gymnasts compete every weekend, 15 to 16 times in four months. The turnaround time for them competitively is unlike anything they have ever experienced. Physically, they spend the entire day after competition in treatment, rehabbing their bodies. They then have two or three days to train before they prepare for the next competition. The day before a competition we either do very light training or give them the day to spend in the athletic training room getting treatment. As much of a change as this is for them physically, every one of our athletes has said the mental game is the most difficult to grasp. Never before in their careers have they had to be "up" for that many meets in a year, let alone every weekend for four months straight.

Tasha Schwikert was a two-time US Olympian and a two-time US national champion. Two months into her freshman year at UCLA she told me, "Miss Val, I love to compete and perform. However, I had no idea it would be this hard to be 'up' weekend after weekend. It's exhausting." I liken it to what Broadway artists must go through having to find a way to be up for eight shows a week, while delivering the same show and keeping it fresh.

As Onnie Willis, a three-time NCAA champion and individual all-around champion, once put it, "Miss Val, college gymnastics may be easier in terms of training hours, but it is much tougher mentally. It is where gymnasts get mentally *buff*."

When Katelyn announced to the team she didn't want to be

great anymore I felt like I'd been sucker punched. My first thought was, "How can any athlete who has experienced so much success now train with the goal of being mediocre?" My next thought was, "Then what are we paying you $62,000 a year for?" And my third thought was, "So what am I supposed to do with this?"

Here was one of our top freshmen, one of the top recruits in the country, revealing that she just didn't want to be great again. At that point another freshman, Nicki Shapiro, spoke up and asked if she could say something about this. Nicki went on to brilliantly deduce that there was nothing positive that Katelyn had ever associated with being great. Every part of what she had experienced those years she trained elite wasn't positive for her. Why would she want to experience that all over again?

Nicki's assessment was spot on. At that moment I realized there was nothing I could say to Katelyn to make her believe that her experience at UCLA would be different. I had to earn her trust, one day at a time. And I honestly had no clue how long it would take. That was one of the most difficult coaching experiences of my career.

Here was this gem of an athlete, extraordinarily talented, physically and mentally gifted, and an unbelievably fierce competitor. And we were getting about 60 percent of her ability because of what she associated with being great.

It took guts for Katelyn to say, "I just don't want to be great again," knowing full well no one was going to be happy with her saying that. She didn't say it for shock value. It was her raw, unapologetic truth. It was one of the most frustrating and respectful conversations I've ever had because I always appreciate brutal honesty, as long as the honesty is stated respectfully. I took a deep breath and decided to stick it out, knowing it was going to take quite some time to turn this situation around.

Had Katelyn not been so honest it's possible she might have been kicked off the team, but I knew she didn't need to be kicked off the team, she needed to experience *trust*. My goal was to create the kind of environment Katelyn needed in order to find her joy in the sport again. It couldn't be forced on her, and we couldn't ask her to fake it. All we could do was work with what we had, which included not allowing her to do skills she wasn't physically fit enough to do. We had to do our best to keep her healthy and contributing to the team's success in the areas in which she was prepared.

During this time I knew I had to show her that I truly cared more about her as a person than as a great athlete. And so, every month or so, I'd ask Katelyn to lunch. Every time we went, I purposefully did not discuss gymnastics and instead asked her about her life, school, boys, family, future goals. I could see the protective shield that she'd put up slowly disintegrate as the lunch went on. And every single time we met, toward the end of the lunch she would bring up gymnastics, which I would happily discuss with the same amount of importance I gave every other topic we discussed—no less and no more.

I wish I had a timeline video of Katelyn's first two years at UCLA. You could literally see her shed her protective shield and watch her inner light and joy shine more brightly with every passing month. By her junior year she was *pure joy*. She was in better physical, mental, and emotional shape than she'd ever been and eagerly shared her life lessons and newfound philosophies with anyone who would listen.

When you watch videos of Katelyn competing in her younger years, you see that she never smiled during her routines, ever. Katelyn's gymnastics was near flawless and gorgeous, and yet her spirit was wilted. Because of her downtrodden demeanor, I'm not sure I would have recruited her had I not had a phone conversation with her during which she shared her feelings so honestly. Katelyn got a second chance to make an impression with that phone call. Had she complained and embraced being a victim, I don't know if I would have recruited her. Instead, she didn't blame anyone, not her coaches or her family. She just explained that she was quitting elite with the hopes of having a positive gymnastics experience before she retired. I respected that and knew I could work with that. In hindsight, I should have realized it would take Katelyn some time to work through her pain before she could fully be an effective team member and leader.

Some of my greatest moments of Katelyn's time at UCLA are when, at some point during every meet, I feel this little hand take mine and Katelyn says, "Come on Miss Val, dance with me." Katelyn has come full circle in finding her joy in the sport that she'd pursued so passionately as a child because she loved it. Katelyn went on to have an amazing junior season, lighting up the arena wherever we competed. In fact, during the 2018 Pac-12 Championships, anchoring the meet for us on floor, Katelyn *lit up* the arena with a spectacular performance that went viral online, and was viewed by over 60 million people. She was an integral part of the Bruins' 2018 NCAA championship win and took home the individual title for floor exercise.

As importantly, Katelyn's life outside the gym is just as bright.

Chapter Eleven

Cultivating Integrity

"Speak with honesty. Think with sincerity. Act with Integrity."

I was recently told by a friend that our program has a different flare than all other gymnastics programs, and the reason why is because I, as the head coach, am an immigrant to the sport of gymnastics. I see gymnastics through a dancer's eye and I have a different vocabulary than most coaches. The culture I've worked to develop at UCLA is one that exemplifies our sport, which is called artistic gymnastics. We seek to perform Big, Beautiful Gymnastics. We are artistic. We are bold. We are elegant. We are poised. We are fun. We offer an athletic "show" in the entertainment capital of the world and offer the best entertainment value for the dollar. It's because we regularly deliver such a high level of athletic showmanship that we average 8,500 fans per home meet. In a city that offers a wide variety of entertainment on any given day, our attendance numbers are phenomenal and they keep getting better.

During our 2017 season we broke our regular meet attendance record with over 12,500 in the stands. An interesting fact is that during the early 2000s we won four championships in five years and our attendance numbers didn't increase. It wasn't until we started producing every aspect of our home events and I started taking control of igniting the crowd, especially the student section, that our numbers started to climb and have kept climbing. Fans want to see a great sporting event, but they also want to be entertained and feel connected.

I remember the first time I told an athlete to run over to the student section to celebrate a great routine. It was Danusia Francis and she had just nailed her bar routine. After she saluted the judge I wove my way in-between all of her teammates who were congratulating her and told her to go high-five the front row of the student section. The students *loved it*! It was magic. The whole arena erupted. At that moment I realized that fans want to be a part of the event. That's why at football games we all stand up and start screaming for our defense to make the stop on the opposing team's third down. We want to know that we matter.

Ever since that moment I've taken control of choreographing how our athletes interact with the crowd and seek to bring the audience into the mix as much as possible. As a result, our attendance numbers and the electric energy in the arena during our meets are undeniably on a whole different level now.

Our team knows that each competition is an entertainment

event. Athletic teams rely on the fans to stay viable and the fans want to be entertained. Suzanne Yoculan has said, "College gymnastics is a performance sport and Valorie has a skill set that attracts performers. I always look at her athletes as more than just gymnasts; they're true performers." That is quite a compliment because our sport is called "artistic gymnastics."

From the time our Bruins walk into Pauley Pavilion arena we have a presence. I want our competitors to feel our kindness. I want every fan and stranger we encounter to appreciate our courtesy. I have been told for years that our athletic trainers love working on our athletes because they always say "Thank you" to whomever is attending them. I want the janitors after the competition to recognize how respectful we are of the facility we're in. This is a culture we cultivate. This is what we honor. This is the character we grow. And my hope is that our student-athletes will transfer these behaviors to their personal lives and homes.

Our team's character is a big reason why half of the last two US Olympic gold medal–winning gymnastics teams have committed to UCLA, including Madison Kocian, Kyla Ross, Jordyn Wieber, and Simone Biles (when Jordyn and Simone both chose to turn pro, they waived their eligibility to compete in the NCAA).

Sheer entertainment can be accomplished easily enough without our athletes reaching their full potential. *That is not our goal.* It's not enough to do Beautiful Gymnastics in a fun atmosphere. We need to do Big Beautiful Gymnastics.

As stated by the Greek philosopher Plato, "What is honored in a country is cultivated there." The same goes for gyms, classrooms, offices, and families. I believe if you want to know the culture of a team, study the head coach's non-negotiables.

If you want to know the true DNA of a team, follow the coaching staff and athletes around all day. What one does some of the time, one does all of the time. It's called integrity. Integrity isn't about being perfect. *Integrity is having perfect intention as regards to your personal mission statement.* Integrity isn't something you can turn on and off depending on what social situation you're in. You either have integrity or you don't. It's like being dead or pregnant. If an athlete's personal mission is to be the best athlete she can be and she has put in an impeccable effort during the time she's in the gym, but then she eats junk food, drinks too much alcohol, and gets little sleep at night, then she doesn't have integrity and her impeccable effort in the gym is wasted. If that's the life she wants to live outside the gym, then to have integrity she should admit, "I just want to be a part-time athlete." That would be having integrity.

I'm extremely proud that we have found a way to support our athletes who not only want to be great collegiate athletes but chose to continue their Olympic dreams while in and after college. We are one of only a few NCAA programs to do this, and we're the only program to train athletes who have made the powerhouse that is the USA women's Olympic gymnastics team *after* they graduated. Mohini Bhardwaj made the 2004 US Olympic team, two years after she graduated from UCLA and was appointed team captain by Martha Karolyi. Anna Li earned the spot of US Olympic alternate for the 2012 team two years after she graduated. In 2010, the high-flying Vanessa Zamarripa became the only woman to make (for the first time) the US national team while simultaneously competing in college, and helping UCLA win championship No. 6 that same year. And Kate Richardson made the 2004 Canadian Olympic team that took place the summer between her sophomore and junior years at UCLA. Interesting and fun fact for me, Kate and Mohini tied for 6th place in floor finals at the 2004 Olympics, both competing floor routines that I had choreographed. I love having our athletes represent UCLA on the international stage. I love hearing how much professionalism, maturity, and poise they bring to their teams.

Over the years I have honed my messages to the team. The girls will say I have a lot of rules, but those rules are meant to instill an awareness in our young women so they represent themselves as they would ideally intend to at all times. Sport is one of the greatest venues to learn life lessons—I repeat this because I believe it. It's not just about winning; and the life lessons take in every bit of minutia.

If our girls are striving for integrity as excellent student-athletes, then they will embody confidence, discipline, courtesy, and civility. It is for this reason that I have certain explicit rules outside of the Golden Rule of *Do unto others as you would have them do unto you*. I fully admit these rules range from super important to seemingly frivolous.

1. **Early is on time. On time is late. (Super Important)** Any time you're meeting someone if you show up at the designated time you're late. When you really care about a meeting you show up early so that you can catch your breath and gather your thoughts before the meeting starts. Being late is rude as it tells the other person that your time is more important than theirs.

2. **No phones at team meals. (Super Important)** I'm doing what I can to help break this horrible habit the smartphone generation has gotten into and accepted. Having your phone out at a restaurant meeting, in an office meeting, or anywhere you are supposed to be engaging in conversation with someone else implies that they don't have your undivided attention. I have yet to be sitting across the table from someone with their phone on the table, even face down, where they don't subconsciously turn it over periodically to check to see if they've missed anything. It's so funny to me now that people are wearing smartwatches; it's exactly the same thing when they check their wrist. It still interrupts the flow of the conversation and signals whomever you're with that they don't have your full, undivided attention.

3. **No gum—ever. (Kinda Super Important)** Gum chewing can become habitual to the point that a person doesn't even know they're putting it in their mouth. Put that right up there with biting one's nails or cuticles, nose picking, or

picking a wedgie. I don't think any of these are things one should do in public. Regarding the gum issue, I want our athletes to be conscious of when they are chewing gum and when they shouldn't: as in public, in an interview, on camera, and so on. I was thrilled when Kate Middleton married Prince William and she had to learn all of the rules for after she joined the ranks of royalty. At the top of the list was no gum. *I loved it!*

4. **No hair ties on your wrist. (Not Important)** This seems like such a silly and insignificant thing. However, if you're a female reading this, think of how often you have a black hair tie on your wrist because "you never know when you'll need it." It has replaced the wristwatch; it is that prevalent. It really isn't offensive, but think about it. If you're in an interview for a job, or on TV, or going to a fancy event, or simply choosing a super fun chic outfit, do you really want a hair tie on your wrist? It's no different than walking around with a pen or pencil behind your ear 24/7 because you never know when you're going to need that. I repeat, it's not offensive; it's just something that you should be conscious of.

5. **No sweatpants dragging on the ground. (Important)** I sympathize with the vertical challenges of most gymnasts. However, if your pants are dragging on the ground, cut them off or get them hemmed. I get as grossly graphic as possible when explaining my reason for this to our team.

When walking from the dorms to the gym they don't know if their pants are dragging in spit, urine, vomit, or dog doo. It's horrifically unsanitary and they bring that filth into the gym, then take it up into their dorm rooms or apartments and it ends up on their beds or even in their beds if they're too lazy to change out of their clothes. And from a polished attire perspective, it looks like we can't afford to outfit our team properly.

6. **No belly or cleavage showing when traveling. (Super Important)** One year we were on a plane loading our bags into the overhead bins when I noticed one of the male passengers already seated in an aisle seat ogling an athlete's bare belly that was exposed when she lifted her bag overhead. I don't necessarily feel the attire was offensive, but it certainly invited unsolicited lechery. No need to encourage ogling.

7. **No bows ever. (Frivolous)** I know that many female athletic teams wear bows. I personally feel that bows are for young girls, not young adult women, and especially not those in an athletic arena. This is a classic case of my team, my rules. The only time I've allowed our team to wear bows is the 2018 season when we opted to wear teal ribbons, the color to show support for the sexual abuse victims. In my opinion that was 100 percent warranted.

8. **No face tattoos. (Frivolous)** I've never understood why teams take beautiful young women and make them less attractive with a face tattoo. I don't believe the face tattoo

makes anyone more attractive. The school logo is already on the uniform. I don't understand this phenomenon. I was particularly peeved during a competition when one of our athletes got a "warning" from a judge to cover the tattoo on her ankle. It was a two-inch tattoo of the Olympic rings. At that time, having tattoos was taboo and a deduction from the athlete's score could be taken. I couldn't help myself as I told the judge, "Time out! The Olympian can't expose the Olympic rings on her ankle because the rules say it's a *distraction*, but that other team can sport fake tattoos on their faces?!? Which is the bigger distraction?"

I'm sure there are more rules like these that I insist upon, but these are the ones that immediately come to mind. I'd like to note that none of these rules are meant to make our team members look like cookie-cutter versions of each other. These rules don't inhibit anyone's personal style.

I actually don't look at these as rules as much as I look at them as "growing up." I figure I have four years with the girls to get them to contemplate how they want to feel about themselves, how they want to be perceived, and what type of a legacy they want to leave at UCLA. My goal is to make them conscious of their choices as early on as possible. Attention to Intention. If they want to show up at a job interview with a hair tie on their wrist and chewing gum that is totally their choice. I just want them to be conscious of that choice.

The culture we try to honor extends to people outside our Bruin Bubble. We do not have closed practices and love when a recruit, family member, someone from the university, or a well-meaning fan shows interest in our hard work and training. I don't expect someone to stop a routine or their rehab to say hello, but if they are not training—and truthfully any given time during our daily training there is always someone who isn't working out for the moment—it is expected that our gymnasts welcome the visitor as if that person were a guest in a home because the gym *is* our home. If someone walks into my home, I don't leave them in the hallway to fend for themselves. I greet them and make them feel welcome. (And if they're not welcome, I'll usher them out.)

It's surprising to me how many of our athletes aren't comfortable introducing themselves to a stranger who happens to walk into our gym, but they learn to do it with grace and kindness. I'm even more amazed as to how many recruits and their parents tell me that our gym is the only gym they've visited where team members came over to greet them and introduce themselves. This is shocking to me! It gets more shocking; I've had recruits recount to me that they visited other team's gyms and no one came over to say hello, not even athletes on the team they'd grown up with!

I totally understand and agree that training time needs to be focused and purposeful, but gymnastics training isn't a team sport where everyone is engaged in activity at exactly the same time. There is always someone available to welcome whoever stops by. Welcoming people is a way to grow support and offer outsiders a peak into the magic behind the scenes, an opportunity most have never experienced. Some might see this as a distraction, but how could it be if our athletes are expected to be able to focus in all different environments? This unique experience for the guest along with the social life skills our athletes hone is a win-win.

Chapter Twelve

Unplugging from Fear

"Everything you've ever wanted is on the other side of fear."

—George Addair

Fear of Missing Out (FOMO) and Fear of Other People's Opinions (FOPO, as coined by famed sport psychologist Michael Gervais) can knock you off your personal course if you let them. We all experience these feelings at some point but if we are aware of them, we can make conscious choices about how to deal with them so the fear doesn't dictate our behavior.

One of the greatest culprits in cultivating both these fears is none other than our smartphones, the device we just can't live without. Remember, in the last chapter, my rule that the athletes can't have their phones with them during a team meal? It's because our habit is to check in with what's happening in our world, a.k.a. FOMO. This in turn starts affecting the team dynamic because they are no longer communicating and connecting with each other.

Information in and about our lives and everything else in the world is streaming instantaneously online. Rather than slow down to reflect, we consume information as quickly as possible and move on to the next thing. During a recent retreat I asked our athletes, "Okay, if you were up at camp for five days without a phone, when you got back would you pick up on today's social media activities or would you go back five days and look at everything you missed while you were away?" Every single one of them said they would have to go back and see everything that they missed. FOMO.

FOMO fills us with anxiety. We worry that we have missed something important. Through FOMO we become more interested in the lives of others than in our own. In fact, fear and separation anxiety from our smartphones are so common these days that researchers have actually given it a name: nomophobia (no-mobile-phone-phobia).

Researchers from the University of Illinois at Urbana–Champaign conducted a study of more than 300 college students and found that those who constantly reached for their smartphone were at greater risk for anxiety and depression, especially those students who used the devices for emotional comfort. They added that this did not apply to those students who reached for their phones out of boredom. In short, if you're already anxious, FOMO on digital information can amplify the problem.

My challenge with this instantly accessible information age is how to deal with it as a coach. I can see that their "relationships" with their phones and the information on those devices put the girls under a tremendous amount of stress because they are unable to step away for any meaningful period of time. I was explaining my concerns to our sports psychologist, Dr. P, in a meeting with the team. He said that the way we use our phones prevents us from listening to and paying attention to what's going on around us. He said, "In order for us to have a conversation with someone, or appreciate the beauty of nature, or enjoy a concert, we need to truly listen." We all agreed with him. Then he said: "To *listen* we need to rearrange those letters…and become *silent*. Not just in terms of speaking, but in our minds." A collective "ahhhhhaaa" filled the room.

In general, what most of us do when others are speaking is to begin formulating what we want to say in response. That is the lowest form of listening. The listen–silent combo is an amazing anagram that can serve as a reminder to quiet the distractions of the modern world. And even harder still, quiet our inner voice enough to just listen.

I believe the best medicine to combat FOMO and FOPO is self-confidence and self-pride. These start with finding your presence and growth from within. As Dr. P has also said, "A person will never see themselves in running water. It is only when the water is still that their reflected image will begin to emerge." So we constantly invite our athletes to be still and quiet in order to discover the beauty within. In fact, we start most workouts by having the girls close their eyes, focus on their breath, and quietly express one thought of gratitude.

One of our coaches, Randy Lane, has noticed something else that is likely related to the ubiquity of the smartphone. For as long as I've been at UCLA, we coaches have always had an open-door policy with our offices. Some of our best teaching moments and some of the most impactful discussions we've had have come about when athletes stopped by just to say hello. Sometimes they'd stop to share something troubling. Other times they just wanted to hang out and possibly take a short nap. Quite often two or more of them would find themselves in our offices and it would end up being a warm, fun time, very much like a close family all sitting around talking about nothing and everything.

Sadly, drop-ins have almost become nonexistent. The only things we can attribute it to are that the girls are no longer bored or, more than likely, they no longer feel they have any free time because all of their actual free time is being used to scroll through social media. Depending on how many people they follow and how many social media platforms they engage in, their opportunities to monitor information is literally endless.

When I shared this theory with one of our alumna, Kristina Comforte, she said, "That is so sad. The most meaningful and insightful discussions I remember having at UCLA were in your office when I just stopped by to say hi."

This means it's more important than ever for me to create opportunities for those moments of connecting by scheduling individual meetings with each athlete. It helps, but a scheduled meeting still lacks the lightheartedness of a drop-in, and often doesn't lead to the organic conversations that come about naturally from just enjoying someone's company when you have sought them out.

Social media has its upsides too. I love being able to go online to see pictures of my family and friends, but I do try to make sure I do so in moderation. I have found though, that while I do not have FOMO, I have been susceptible to FOPO.

A few years ago I felt compelled to read a few of the online gymnastics message boards. People on the message boards may be snarky and hurtful at times, but they are usually extremely knowledgeable, intelligent, and in-the-know about what's going on in the gymnastics world. In fact, they typically know more about what's going on in gymnastics than I do. Therefore, I felt it was a great place to glean information about recruits, find out what other teams were doing well, and see how we were being perceived. It was the worst year of my coaching career. I got some serious FOPO. The decisions I made with my team that year were fueled by a desire to have positive online comments rather than what I actually felt was best for our team. I realized that to spend time on message boards or other social media explaining and qualifying my decisions was not only a huge drain on my time, but it was stifling my enthusiasm for my vision and my work. So I decided to quit cold turkey. No more message boards. No more outside input.

As good as it was to shed my dependence on other opinions, this was a classic case of a pendulum swinging too far in the opposite direction. Now I had *no* input or barometer besides my own perception of reality. This proved to be equally bad.

Today I've come up with a solution that allows me to get brutally honest feedback without getting sucked into the dark recesses of the internet. I have a few select vetted gym nerds (a term of endearment of their own creation) that I will reach out to when I need fresh eyes and an unbiased reality check. Their insight is priceless, as is their trust and confidentiality.

I recently realized that the gym nerds with whom I consult all have an innate appreciation for diversity and aren't judgmental of things that go against the status quo. It was pointed out to me that I have a large cadre of gay men in my gym nerd circle. When asked why, the answer was instantly very clear. While some of my gay male friends can be snarky and judgmental, they are *all* quick to listen, and have no problem changing their opinions, if warranted. I can't help but think this stems from their own personal experiences of coming out and just wanting to be listened to with an open heart and mind.

I can look back on my life and career and see very clearly that I have almost always chosen to challenge the status quo, think outside the box, and take risks. When you can openly express yourself, you're unabashedly able to release your artistry and innovation, not fearing outside judgment. Changemakers are the ones willing to take the hits and public ridicule in order for something fresh to be cultivated.

So, what does artistry even look like in athletics? It's college football coach Chip Kelly crafting an offense in Oregon that no one has ever seen before. In basketball, it's Kareem Abdul Jabbar coming up with the *skyhook* that proved impossible to defend. In gymnastics it's Nastia Liukin adding an arabesque after a kick-over front flip on beam. In business, it's Steve Jobs, it's Elon Musk, it's Uber, it's Amazon. It's an individual altering our thoughts on how their craft can be executed. These breakthroughs weren't found in any "sports bible." They required the vision of individual artists, which is vital for innovation.

What solidifies an artist's place in the pantheon of greats is that they are able to get us to see things with fresh eyes and appreciate their genius *even if we don't like it*. When an artist is able to do this we either proclaim them genius and their resulting work a masterpiece or we're quick to judge and proclaim our righteous opinion. Many times throughout my coaching career, my athletes and I have been on the receiving end of strong opinions when we have dared to do something new and different.

A vivid memory of this happened in 2005 with Ariana Berlin. Having been in the dance troupe Culture Shock, Ariana was a performance trifecta: gymnast, hip-hop dancer, and break-dancer. I allowed her to compete a revolutionary hip-hop and break-dancing floor routine. Other examples were my designing an open-back leotard for our athletes and my being a fool to encourage former British national team member Danusia Francis to compete one of the hardest beam dismounts in the world even though she didn't need it to score well in college. In fact, because the move was so difficult, Danusia often got a deduction for waiting too long before executing it. And still, we opted to keep it in for the sake of artistic gymnastics. I love the fact that we stayed the course and didn't cave to FOPO.

And, I don't know if it was because we kept chipping away at tightening up the time she waited between her dance and executing the dismount, or if the judges finally started appreciating the uniqueness and difficulty of the skill, but to close out her career at UCLA, in her senior year, Danusia became the national balance beam champion with that signature dismount.

I have the hardest time understanding why people feel the need to be harshly critical and judgmental of something just because it's *new*. When I encounter something new, unless it's harmful to someone else, I always think, "This is soo cool. Innovation, once again!"

I am proud to say that I have learned to not succumb to FOPO. In fact, I can't remember the last time I got nervous to speak in front of people; I learned early on that making mistakes, which I do often on stage, only endears me more to my audience. However, in 2016 I literally thought I was going to freeze like a deer in headlights or throw up. What actually happened? I honestly don't remember. What I do know is that Valeri Liukin, father of Olympic gold medalist Nastia Liukin; Mike Rawlings, the mayor of Dallas; Madison Kocian, Olympic gold medalist (and at that time incoming Bruin); and Laurent and Cecile Landy, Madison's coaches, and a couple hundred guests watched me stand on a stage and rap a cappella.

Let me put this in context. I was asked to speak at a celebration in honor of Madison Kocian's part in the US Olympics women's gymnastics team's gold medal performance in Rio. I knew there would be other speakers who would give memorable praise to Madison. I wanted to give her something different, and since I had just seen the Broadway hit *Hamilton* I decided to write her a rap. No, I'm not a songwriter, let alone a rap artist. I'm not even that big of a rap fan. I wrote and rewrote for a solid two weeks and practiced until it flowed. I was ready. It was different from the standard congratulations speech, but since I was paying homage to Madison in a respectful way, I was comfortable with my choice. That is until I entered the ballroom where the event was taking place. Panic!!!

I didn't hear one word of what the first two speakers said. All I heard was my heart beating loudly and my inner voice having an argument: "Don't do it." "You have to do it." "Nope, you don't have to do it, you can just give a normal congratulations speech. It will be simple and lovely." "Stop being a wuss. Who cares if some people think it's stupid? You wrote it as a gift to Madison, to show her that her new adventure with you and UCLA gymnastics is going to be filled with exciting and character-building challenges." "Nope, nope, nope, I can't do it."

Then . . . I walked up to the podium.

I took a deep breath and decided to take the chance, the leap into sheer terror. I can't tell you if I performed my lines correctly or if people applauded or booed. My heart was literally pounding too loudly.

What was I afraid of? What made me, a regular speaker and a person familiar with making a fool of myself—and a master of not caring—panic? I think it was the fear of the unknown. I had no idea how I was going to be received. I preach all the time that we should be able to say anything to anyone as long as we're being honest and respectful. I was being totally honest and respectful in my rap; it was my personal gift to Maddie. I was worried that the mayor and/ or Madison's coaches would feel I wasn't taking the event seriously. But quite the contrary, I took it very seriously and had prepared 10 times more for this than I usually do for a speech. I had prepared something that I'd intended as a special gift for someone I greatly respected. Why did I care what anyone else would think of my gift?

Because it was different. Because it was outside of the normal. Because I wanted a "sure thing." Because I didn't want to be made fun of, I had a serious attack of FOPO.

Even though I don't have any recollection of how it went, I'm glad I did it. I'm glad I gave Madison something unique. I'm glad I showed all of the young people who were there that you *can* take chances and be different from other people. That "different" can be awesome and fun. So without further ado, here's my rap to Madison:

> *Her name is Madison Kocian.*
> *The latest WOGA locomotion.*
> *A long line of . . . tough-minded, steel-hearted kids with a soul*
> *Who put their blinders on and aim for one goal.*
> *The athletes may change but the message is consistent*
> *When you represent WOGA, you learn to be persistent.*
> *The chance to represent her country with pride*
> *her family, her coaches, and her fans worldwide.*
> *She could feel it in her soul, a fire red-hot*
> *No injury or politics will keep her from her SHOT.*

She is not one to sit and wonder "what if";

She takes charge of her life so don't give her no lip.

Her name is Madison Kocian.

You see she has this magic potion.

Built from… devotion and emotion and a coach with a clear notion

She took her mad skills and won across every ocean.

She turned Red, White, and Blue into Silver and Gold.

She helped shock the World

Our girls broke the mold.

She is the M-A-D-I-S-O-N

K-O-C-I-A-N.

She's got beauty, she's got brains, she's got talents off the chart

She's a pint-sized warrior with a champion's heart.

So what now??? No worries no doubts… you see…

She is conditioned to find a new mission

She doesn't need our permission.

She's a national, world, and Olympic champion and someday soon… a pediatrician. From Dallas to LA, from medals to a ring

She might even find a guy who makes her heart sing.

Maddie you're a star. Your light shines bright.

From your youth you've impressed with your keen insight.

Now, I'm the luckiest coach alive cuz I get to say

"I get to coach Maddie at UCLA."

I do have one confession. I chickened out in asking someone to record it. I was worried I would be reminded of my humiliation. To rectify this, I performed my rap a second time and posted it on my website for the entire world to see. I know I can't get away with acting cool, and I'm not a rap artist, but I can live knowing I dropped the fear and then dropped the mic. Boom.

Chapter Thirteen

Diverse Not Divisive

"I'm not concerned with your liking or disliking me...all I ask is that you respect me as a human being."

—JACKIE ROBINSON

At the end of our 2016 season, 1984 Olympic gold medalist Bart Connor said to me, "You have the most diverse team." I looked at our team and realized he was right.

"Yes, we're like the United Nations," I replied.

- Danusia Francis: Jamaican and Polish, looks black but has blond hair that she wears proudly plumed on top of her head.
- Sadiqua Bynum: Black with a fierce mohawk.

- Sophina DeJesus: Puerto Rican and black with a massive died blue fluffy pony tail.
- Christine "Peng-Peng" Lee: Chinese Canadian with her signature double buns.
- Angi Cipra: Hispanic with slicked-back black shiny hair.
- Mikaela Gerber: One of the few blond Anglo-Saxons.

"I'm not talking about their ethnicity," he explained. "I'm talking about how you encourage them to develop and celebrate their own personal style." Then he said, "Your team proves that celebrating diversity can actually be unifying instead of divisive." That was the greatest compliment I have ever received as a coach.

The reason Bart's comment was the ultimate compliment for me was because my overarching job with the athletes in my care is to help them develop into the best versions of themselves in the short time they're with our program. I have always believed that if I can help them be healthy mentally, emotionally, and physically, then their gymnastics will be amazing. The opposite approach is to focus on their gymnastics and hope it will take care of their overall health and well-being. I've learned that one can only truly shine in all of those areas when they are fueling their own uniqueness and not trying to be anyone else.

Research has shown that when we are with people who look and think like we do, we tend to emphasize our similarities. However, when we're in a more diverse group we feel freer to openly express our uniqueness. Isn't this great?! So if you want to get the most out of yourself and the people around you, hang out with all sorts of people, keep an open mind, compliment everyone's unique traits that enhance our planet, and let the light of your difference shine brightly.

When you think about it, diversity, at its core, is the most natural thing in the world. To thrive, Mother Nature depends on biodiversity, with plants and animals all nourishing each other.

The diversity I have injected into this sport extends to what our athletes wear—and I've been told by many gymnastics fans that this book would not be complete if I didn't discuss our leotards. Yes, you read that correctly. Leotards. I honestly don't see what the big deal is, but like other unorthodox things I've done with our team, I've pushed the creative envelope with our competition attire.

I've always loved fashion and I've marveled at the musculature of a gymnast's body. My goal has always been to blend the two in innovative and interesting ways. I will flip through fashion magazines to get inspirations for how I want our gymnasts to look in the competition arena.

Once I see a dress I like I relay that information to Candy Dengrove of Rebecca's Mom Leotards who has crafted our leotards for over two decades. Some of our past designs have been major hits, and some are miserable misses. The ones I like best are the ones where I have asked 10 different people their opinions and half have said, "Love them" and half have said, "I hate them, burn them now." I don't know why, I just love the controversy they can stir up, and how passionately vehement people's opinions about a leotard can get.

One of the most talked about designs we've come up with is the open-back leotard. We first wore them in competition in the mid-90s and everybody, including leotard-manufacturing companies Alpha Factor and GK Elite, wanted to know how our gymnasts were wearing them—specifically how were they wearing them without bras? We had two secret weapons: great design by Candy and my personal history with and understanding of how to perform in backless attire for dance; you use a half bra made from stretchy athletic tape.

Legendary Georgia coach Suzanne Yoculan has said she would never have put her gymnasts in an open-back leotard; she has referred to them as "dancer-style" leotards. Suzanne was a fierce competitor and she wanted her gymnasts to look and feel like athletes. I had to chuckle when I heard this because it says so much about our different styles—with similar goals. While she would not have chosen backless leotards because she wanted her athletes to feel like super-athletes, I deliberately chose to put our athletes in backless leotards for this exact same reason. The leotards show off the gymnasts' extraordinary muscular backs. If I had their back muscles, I'd go backless every day of my life!

The greatest compliment I've had concerning our leotard designs happened when I was sitting in the stands at the 2012 Olympic Games in London and out marched the Russian gymnastics team in our *exact* leotard design. At first, I admit, I didn't know whether to be pissed or excited. But, because I do believe that imitation is the greatest form of flattery, I chose to be flattered and couldn't wait to call Candy and tell her that her leotard design was an international hit.

While I will continue to push the creative envelope with our attire so that we can maintain a visual point of difference that ignites an audience—in addition to our routines, of course!—I also encourage our athletes to find their own unique looks for our competitions. Sadiqua Bynum took it upon herself—with my encouragement—to undergo one of the biggest visual transformations I've experienced, and to own a radically untraditional hairstyle for competitions that I believe has challenged all gymnastics mores.

In her freshman year, I pointed out to Sadiqua that she was a naturally, physically strong woman with a big, compassionate heart. A lot of people only saw her as a magnificent, muscular, beautiful black woman but didn't see her artistry. I wanted Sadiqua to have something visual that showed her strength but that was also artistically beautiful. I encouraged her to do something with her hair that was unique to her personality. I immediately suggested a faux hawk—taking her hair and pulling it up in the middle so it referenced a Mohawk. It's a sleek, fierce, and commanding look that conveys strength and control without being harsh. Sadiqua tried it out and told the audience at the awards banquet wrapping up our 2016 season that when she styled her faux hawk for meets, she felt empowered. Sadiqua eventually had her hair shaved into a real Mohawk and fully embraced the look; regardless of whether or not the gymnastics community approved, Sadiqua went on to earn All-American honors.

"In high school I had a different life from everyone else," Sadiqua has told me. "I'm black and I was adopted and have white parents, so I always felt 'different.' Coming here, I tried to find myself by trying to fit in. You gave me permission to set myself apart. To not try to be black or white, but just be me. You were also the one who allowed me to embrace my natural hair." At the banquet Sadiqua also said that she felt like she'd finally arrived at being the person she was supposed to become. She said that owning her presentation gave her a courage and confidence she'd never felt before.

This is part of the UCLA gymnastics brand. Be who you are and continue to develop who you are until the day you die. In order to feel empowered you have to do you. So many times we try to impersonate someone else whom we admire; it's not wrong, it just doesn't do anything to help you develop into your real *you*.

I want to stress that I don't let all self-expression fly. This is where I can come across as hypocritical. I'll explain. We are part of a team and there are parameters to one's self-expression. The main parameter being whether or not I approve. My feeling is that we are all representing UCLA gymnastics and I am the leader of the program. I have the ultimate say in what represents the story of our brand.

In 1997 we had a brilliant Hawaiian neuroscience student, Kiralee Hayashi, on the team. Kiralee came in to the gym over the summer of her sophomore year sporting short blue spikey hair. I told her I didn't think it was a good look on her and so I asked what her thoughts were on the hairstyle—what was her intention? She said she was just trying to assert herself. She said, "Miss Val, I don't drink, I don't do drugs, I don't sloppy kiss. If this is the worst it gets it's not that bad." I didn't force her to change her hair right away, but I did tell her that this wasn't a "look" I was excited to showcase in promoting our team. I told her she had a myriad of natural colors to choose from and to pick one by the time the recruits arrived in October. A few weeks later she came back with blonde spikes instead of blue. I felt it accomplished her need to assert herself and my desire to have our athletes present themselves in a manner that enhances their beauty rather than detracts from it.

In 2015 Sophina DeJesus decided that her signature look would be a massively curly, dark *blue* ponytail. I approved. Why did I approve that and not Kiralee's choice? In my opinion, Kiralee's full head of blue hair wasn't flattering to her. The fact that Sophina chose to color just parts of her ponytail gave her hairstyle some flare. I didn't exactly love it, but I didn't dislike it enough to veto it. It's the same way I feel about our young women wearing double buns. I think they look great on little girls, but not on young women; still, I don't hate it.

One style I've not softened on is cornrows. For some reason, I feel that they create a really "hard look" for anyone who wears them, men and women alike. Personally, I've just never been a fan. One day Jeanette Antolin came in with cornrows. I didn't say anything to her about them, so halfway through the workout she asked me if I liked them. I told her "No."

She asked, "Why not?" I told her I didn't think it was a flattering look on her. It made her look very "harsh" and not necessarily in a good, fierce way. She came back with, "It's a free country, I can wear my hair however I want."

I said, "Yes, you can. And just as Coach Wooden told Bill Walton many years ago when he showed up for practice with his hair hanging down past his neck, 'I'm the head coach of this team and you can wear your hair anyway you'd like to, but you won't be on the floor, you'll be sitting in the stands.'" Just as Bill rushed into Westwood (the campus neighborhood) to get a haircut, Jeanette came in the next day without cornrows. The reason Coach Wooden didn't let his players have long hair was because of the potential for sweat to get in their eyes from their hair. My reason with the cornrows: I just don't like them.

I had a similar experience with Katelyn Ohashi during her sophomore season. She also showed up to a meet with her hair in cornrows. While she and the team were warming up on beam, I explained to her that while I appreciated her wanting to express her individuality, I didn't think this was a flattering look for her. During warm-ups I started picking the cornrows out of her hair. I thoroughly appreciated the fact that she let me do it right there on the competition floor as she was warming up. She even took a warm-up turn on the beam with half of the cornrows in and half out. There is no way this transaction would have happened so easily or unemotionally had Katelyn and I not developed a relationship of trust; she knows I always have her best interests and not my ego at heart.

One more point I'd like to make about visual presentation during a competition is this: "If you can see the audience, the audience can see you." It's a quip I've borrowed from the theatre. It particularly applies to something that drives me crazy: it's when our athletes roll "butt glue" on their bums so their leotards will stay down. They have done this while standing on the arena floor, right before they salute the judge to perform on an event! The gymnasts honestly aren't considering the fact that they are lifting up the backsides of their leotards and exposing their "cheeks" in front of thousands of people.

This thoughtlessness is taken to a whole other level when you consider nearly everyone nowadays has a smartphone and can take a "cheek" shot and post it for all the world to see. I have had many discussions over the years about people's perception based on your presentation. Many times I hear things like "It's my life and I don't care how I look to someone else." The point is just that. It *is* your life and you can present yourself any way you want. You just can't be naïve enough not to think that someone's perception of you is not their *reality* of you. Moreover it's unrealistic to think someone will take pause and give you the benefit of the doubt that you are different than how you present yourself.

Chapter Fourteen

The Power of Choice

"Champions are made when no one else is watching."

—Unknown

I'm a super visual person. When I think of taking charge of everything I think and do, I see a spotlight shining on each of the
choices I make. As I'm going through my day, my spotlight isn't
focused on someone else, it's smack dab on me everywhere I go, spot-
lighting every single choice I make. If you think about how we are
free to design, craft, choreograph, and own our lives, the spotlight
visual becomes a mesmerizing one. Imagine the spotlight leaving
behind a trail of light that highlights all the consequences that come
from any one choice you make. When I consider this, sometimes I
want the light to shine even brighter because I'm so proud of the ini-

tial choice I made that set into action such amazing things. Other times I wish I had a massive magic eraser so I could go undo the light trail of consequences as well as the initial choice that sparked them.

It's not just about the immediate repercussion from the initial choice we make. The interesting part is when you follow that one choice through to everything that happens subsequently…its compound or ripple effect is boundless.

Every year I have a talk with the girls on the team to demonstrate how even the most passive and seemingly insignificant of choices has an impact on their lives and the lives of others. The girls call it "Miss Val's Circle of Life."

I focus on the six most significant things they go through almost every day as a college student and athlete: morning gymnastics training, class, studying, nutrition, socializing, and sleep.

I draw a circle and point to the top. It's 11:00 p.m. and you can *choose* to wind down and go to sleep knowing you've got to be in the training room for 6:30 a.m. athletic treatment in preparation for 8:00 a.m. gym training. But Hot Football Guy stops by and wants to walk into Westwood to get an In-N-Out burger because he's being asked to put on weight by his coaches. Sleep or take a short trip with Hot Guy? Very easy decision. Hot Guy, of course. I can sleep tomorrow night.

That one choice has now set in motion a chain of reactions that will most likely have numerous negative consequences.

So you're in Westwood and realize it's silly and maybe even a little awkward to let Hot Guy eat alone. You make the disciplined choice to not get a burger and shake but instead opt for a few harmless french fries. No damage done. You enjoy your night and get back to your dorm at 1:00 a.m.

Unfortunately, the maximum hours of sleep you can now get is down to four—plus you've just added at least 200 unwanted, unneeded, sabotaging calories that just erased the cardio you did earlier in the day. No big deal in the grand scheme of things, you'll get back on track tomorrow.

With only four hours to sleep you wait until the last minute to jump out of bed, which means you didn't have time to get something for breakfast. No food and very little sleep also mean you're not exactly in a perky mood, excited to get started accomplishing your goals for the day.

You make it to the gym on time and go through training, not excited or motivated, but going through the motions, just trying to get through the day without calling attention to the fact you're exhausted. Needless to say you don't have a great day in the gym.

Unlike yesterday when you were prepared, today you aren't helping your teammates. You don't have the energy to show your best or to motivate others, and you certainly aren't adding any positive energy to the gym. Again, no problem; you can fake a few smiles and high fives and get back on track tomorrow.

You rush out of the gym and sit down in class and feel pretty good that you at least showed up—even though you're not paying attention and are therefore not learning anything. When you sit down later to study the information presented in class, it will be harder to absorb and understand because it will be the first time you're paying attention to it. Did I mention your lack of nutrition and sleep has made you poopy, pissy, grumpy, and every other adjective that describes your tired apathetic mood?

Lunchtime. Crap. I forgot to pick up the lunch that our nutritionist provides for us each day because I was foggy-brained. That's okay. I'll get a Jamba Juice. It's quick and healthy, right? If you count 45 grams of sugar as healthy; it's nearly twice the daily recommendation.

You think, "Okay, I have a choice" and really decide to get back on track. That means sleep to refresh the body and mind. However, the only time you can "spare" during the day for a nap is when you're supposed to be in tutoring. Problem solved. You'll get the notes from a friend. A nap is more important. A quick nap, then a healthy dinner, then some studying before a decent bedtime.

But, ohhh, check you out. You run into Hot Guy again on your way back to the dorms. "Sure, I'd love to go into Westwood with you to get something to eat." After all, you do have to eat dinner right?

And on and on and on, around you go in the Circle of Life. While I'd love to blame Hot Guy for this unfortunate circle of pain, it's not Hot Guy's fault you've spun the circle's momentum in the direction that takes you away from your goals of doing well in school and helping your team earn a national championship title. It's *your* choices—every single one of them—that have an impact on whether you're moving toward or away from your goals.

The good news? The Circle of Life spins in both directions. By simply deciding *not* to go out that fateful night, you start a positive circle of consequences: you are getting enough sleep, waking in time to get breakfast, and are not feeling poopy and pissy. You are actually feeling good and enjoying your teammates, which leads to a good day in the gym. You remember to grab the nutritious lunch and are alert to learning something in class. Whether you have time for a wee nap or not your tutoring is productive, making the upcoming test that much easier and less stressful, which sets you up for an even better day tomorrow. And Hot Guy is actually *more* interested in you now because you're independent, have goals and aspirations and the discipline to achieve them, and you don't *need* him, which makes you that much more attractive to him. Again…a win-win.

It may seem like a lot to ask, but no matter what choices they are making, I expect our athletes to show up in the gym every day feeling inspired and energetic. We coaches show up inspired every day and expect no less from the athletes. One of the trademarks that defines our team is our zealous enthusiasm. You can walk into our gym at any time starting at 7:45 a.m. and feel the pulsating energy; it's a fun, positive, inspired environment. This is something our coaching staff and I take great pride in. We consciously take responsibility for establishing the positive energy in the gym from the moment we step into the building. As the girls file in for training they are greeted with a spirited "Good morning" from us. If any of them scoot on by with a less than bright and cheerful response we check in with them to see if everything is okay. If it's not, we take the opportunity to help them work through whatever is upsetting them.

If it turns out that they haven't fully woken up yet and are just pissy, we call them over and give a pep talk about how important it is that we all contribute to and appreciate the positive and excited energy in the gym. It may seem like a lot to ask of them every day but then again, if we coaches can show up inspired every day, then so can they. Plus, I don't want them doing potentially dangerous gymnastic skills if they have a negative or uninspired attitude. If they can't turn it around, then they're instructed to take a personal day.

Personal days (PDs) are my way of giving the girls a voice and choice. As I've said, my definition of a coach is someone who motivates change. You can get someone to do what you tell them to do, but to motivate them to want to do something is tricky. Each of us is motivated by different things, and we can't assume that what motivates one person will motivate another. I like to start with empowerment and PDs are a great tactic.

Each student-athlete is given three PDs a quarter that they can take whenever they want. I started this because I was tired of questioning some of the girls' excuses as to why they weren't in gym on any particular day; quite often I felt they were lying. Sometimes we all just need a day to get our life back on track. For our girls it's usually to get their laundry done, sleep in, study for an exam, or finish a paper. The beauty of the PD is that they don't need my approval to take a day off (the only caveat is that they can't take a PD on days we have intra-squads—internal team competitions—or team meetings). I feel this has (all but) eliminated their need to lie to me. I do know it has helped them with time-management skills because the first thing they do each quarter is go through their class schedules and plan out their PDs around their exams.

One year Jeanette Antolin, who was into fashion, laughed as she told me she was going to take a PD to go to the LA Fashion District for a jeans sale. I said, "Wow fabulous!" and to show her I was serious, I asked if she would keep an eye out for some fabulous jeans in my size.

Another way we encourage our athletes to take charge of their own well-being is through our daily tracking sheet. This is one of the greatest tools we've devised since we've had gymnasts of nearly all competitive skill levels and accomplishments come through the program, and is something we learned from the University of Utah. In the 1980s Dr. Bill Sands was one of their assistant coaches. He is revered as one of the most brilliant science minds that has ever coached our sport. He developed a tracking sheet for the Utes and we took it and tweaked some things that fit well into our Bruin program. To make sure we take care of our athletes, I work with our entire staff. In particular, I work with Lorita Granger, our head athletic trainer, to determine what is the best approach for each athlete *each day*.

The whole purpose of the tracking sheet is to help prevent injury. It is a compilation of daily data that helps us make better choices about how to coach each individual athlete. Each morning our athletes record how much sleep they've gotten, how they're feeling with regard to injuries or illness (ranked 0–10, 10 being extremely painful), and what they've eaten for breakfast. Once our athletes start warming up, Lorita goes over the tracking sheet with our coaching staff. It may go something like, "Madison Kocian's shoulder pain is staying the same, so I think we should keep her training on bars to every other day." Or "Check out Sonya's amount of sleep: 3 hours." At which point I'll go check in with Sonya Meraz to see what the problem is. This check-in has illuminated a wide variety of issues from perpetual sleep disturbances to anxiety over school to roommate issues to being homesick, and so on.

The tracking sheet is by no means an absolute measure of what's going on with each athlete, but it gives us a peek into how they're feeling that day. If there are red flags on the tracking sheet, we will opt for that athlete to take a day off or just do conditioning. It's not worth the risk of an athlete getting injured because they're not feeling up to par. I would rather have them take off a day of training than have to sit out an entire year due to an injury that could have been prevented.

I'm not naïve enough to think that every gymnast tells the full and complete truth on the tracking sheet. It's their choice what to say. I'm not surprised to find out later that a gymnast lied on the tracking sheet about how much sleep she got, because it turns out she stayed out all night. The important thing is that there are no punitive damages. It is solely about the health and well-being of the athletes. It has been hard at times to not get on an athlete who consistently gets three to four hours a sleep a night, especially when I know they're making poor choices. However, if there were "punishments" associated with the tracking sheet then there would be a lot more false reporting. As it stands, the number of hours of sleep they confess to is usually something we highly suspect anyway. (If you're one of our athletes reading this right now, I know you're laughing and agreeing.)

To further empower the choices of our student-athletes, and to strengthen their art of diplomacy, we have devised a personal challenge mechanism called the "Blue Light Special." I don't remember when we started doing this, but the athletes love it. Basically it gives them an avenue to learn the art of negotiation, compromise, and accountability. Each day we coaches have specific assignments for the athletes on each event. For example, the balance beam assignment could be to hit "3 naty quality pod rounds." Let's break down what that means. A "pod" stands for three athletes. Each of them has to hit a national championship quality routine, one right after the other. Once each of the three hits a quality routine they will have completed one round. They have do this three times. If the pod is having a hard time getting through the assignment, they can come up with a Blue Light Special, which means they can offer an alternate assignment *and* the consequences if they don't successfully complete it.

It *never* fails that the girls get all excited formulating the new assignment, but they always forget to suggest the consequences. Their reaction is always the same: supreme enthusiasm for "selling me" on the new compromise and a bit of a slump when they remember that they have to come up with the consequences.

I *love* the Blue Light Special concept because it puts their gymnastics (and their teammates') smack dab in the middle of their accountability box. I always know our team has turned the corner to becoming champions when they take ownership of their team dynamic *and* their accountability. This isn't just about gymnastics, of course. The gymnasts are learning to find confidence in their own voice and strength in their decisions.

The Blue Light Special also helps those who are exceptional to push themselves when they might otherwise get bored or slowed down. Kyla Ross, a member of the 2012 Fierce Five gold medal Olympic team frequently calls for a Blue Light Special. "I really enjoy the Blue Light Special because it gives us a chance to decide our own outcome while challenging us at the same time," Kyla told me. "It is a great exercise that creates a high-pressure situation similar to that in a competition. I believe having games in the gym that challenge us mentally and physically is what makes us stronger and tougher athletes."

Even though there are Olympians and world champions in our program I still don't consider myself a coach in the traditional sense. (Fun fact: current Bruins Kyla Ross and Madison Kocian are the only two female gymnasts on the planet who have won Olympic gold, world championship gold, and NCAA national titles.) So it's probably not surprising that I have made up my own rules and reasons for what our team should do the night before a competition.

For years our pregame preparation has taken place the night before (not the day of) the competition and always focuses on getting the team loose by having fun and connecting with each other.

The last thing I want to do the night before a meet is to have them stress out about the next day's competition and not have them sleep. We do daily mental routines during the course of the year and up the numbers as we get closer to championship season. The day before a competition, during our on-site training we include mental routines on each event. By the time we leave the arena that day our training is over; it's time to enjoy each other and keep the spirits positive and energy loose.

As I've previously mentioned, everything we do with the team is intentional. It may seem like the games I'm about to share with you are fluff, but there are a definite intention and a desired result behind each one. Our overall goal is to keep the team bonded, positive, and loose. Here are a few of my favorite pregame activities.

Performance Art

We divide the team into their classes, freshmen through seniors. Each class has to create a performance around the UCLA alma mater. The rules are that everyone has to sing. They have to use interpretive dance. And, they have to use a form of sign language (that they make up).

Jordyn Wieber's freshmen year was by far the most memorable. She and her classmates, Hallie Mossett, Angi Cipra, Mikaela Gerber, and Alex Waller, started singing the anthem in a traditional manner. Shortly into their act Jordyn's phone rang…everyone froze. Jordyn forgot to turn off her phone during a team meeting!!! *Major faux pas!!!* Everyone stopped for her to answer it. Awkward silence for poor Jo. I'll never forget her seriously speaking into the phone, "Hello? John? John Wooden? You want us to do what? An updated version of the Alma Mater? Okay. Sure, no problem. Got it, Coach. Love you! Bye." As she hung up her classmates dropped a beat and they turned the alma mater into a rap. Everyone went crazy! (This was after Coach had passed, which made her phone call idea even more ingenious.)

The objective here is to give the girls opportunities to learn how to "perform." We often talk about putting the athletes in an uncomfortable situation so they can learn how to make themselves comfortable in that—and any—situation. This exercise also serves to bond them together and gives everyone a voice in helping to make up the performance. This particular exercise also encourages the girls to learn the words to their alma mater, which infuses them with even more school pride.

Blue versus Gold Trivial Pursuit

This one is really a great way to pump up our team pregame; it reminds them of everything they've accomplished that year. We play this game toward the end of the season when we've got stats that will impress and excite them, such as:

- "How many teammates have scored a 9.95 or higher on any event this season?"
- "Which teammate has the most 9.9s?"
- "How many weeks have we been ranked No. 1 on floor?"

- "How many different Bruins have competed for us this year?"
- "How many Bruins have recorded a personal best on an event this year?"

We like to use stats that don't just showcase the superstars but also include stats that illuminate a team member who doesn't get much acknowledgment. This game always has the same great result: it gets the team to feel excited, supportive of each other, and invincible.

Our objective is to get them to realize how much they've accomplished and to celebrate more people than just the ones who always get the recognition.

The Great Debate

This is one of our favorites because it serves many purposes. The team is divided into two groups, Blue and Gold, our school colors. Each athlete gets a topic and must debate the importance of that topic in front of the rest of the team. Some examples:

- Convince us why UCLA should become a nudist campus.
- Discuss why UCLA should change its name to UC-La.
- Discuss the benefits of starting each sentence with "What, Why..."
- Discuss why everyone in the world should shave their heads bald.

- Discuss why curling is the most intense Olympic sport.
- Discuss the best way to remove, clean, cook, and serve frog eyeballs.
- Discuss the benefits of majoring in Silence.

The girls get judged and scored based on a number of elements: the length of their debate (it cannot exceed 90 seconds); making eye contact with the audience; deductions for every instance they say "like" or "um"; and a requirement to properly conjugate an SAT word in their argument. Of course, they are also judged and scored on the content and persuasiveness of their argument as well as their overall presentation.

The judges are usually UCLA support staff who travel with us, including our sports information director, our athletic director, our athletic trainer, and our director of operations. And just like the judges from *Dancing with the Stars*, our judges give each competitor a score from 1 to 10 and provide reasons for their scores.

It would be wonderful to be able to have time for media and public speaking training with our athletes, but their gym and school schedules don't leave much opportunity for this. So, we get creative with our time on the road together and craft challenges like *The Great Debate* to give them experience speaking in front of people they are comfortable with and in an environment where they aren't afraid to make mistakes. It is remarkable to see the growth in their public speaking chops from one year to another. No exaggeration, Katelyn Ohashi couldn't get through the first 10 seconds of her debate her freshman year without totally cracking up. On a scale of 1–10, when most of her teammates' lowest scores were 8s and 9s, Katelyn was receiving 3s. She would have us all cracking up with her, but I couldn't believe that someone who was such a great gymnastics competitor couldn't get through 10 seconds of public speaking without totally losing it. By her sophomore year she was a pro. Her transformation in this area has given her the confidence to start a blog and participate in open mic events reading her poetry. She is also in the process of producing a podcast.

The fact that we can help our student-athletes learn valuable life skills through our time together as an athletic team is extremely important to me.

One of my favorite examples of witnessing a person blossom was the moment Anna Li decided to take charge of her life. Anna was one of our superstars. It was September of her senior year. We were up in Tehachapi, California, at Woodward, our train-away camp. Anna was giving me the same sob story I'd heard for the past four years (even before she was at UCLA and still in high school). "Miss Val, I don't understand why I don't have any real good girlfriends," she said. "No one on the team likes me. I'm just so sad all the time. Why is life so hard?"

We were walking from the cafeteria to the theater room for a team meeting, and I simply said, "Anna, it's time you Choose Happy. Right now, this moment, change your life." I snapped my fingers.

"Choose to be happy," I went on. "Choose to think about the positive things and all of the blessings that you have. Right now. Choose happy."

The next few steps, we took in silence. It was obvious Anna was on the cusp of what would be one of the biggest turning points in her life. She turned to me and simply said, "Okay."

From that moment on, Anna was a totally different person. She was happy. Her teammates absolutely loved her. She was fun. She was the absolute team leader. She was thriving for the first time in her life—all because she *chose* to take charge of her thoughts, her emotions, her life. She *chose happy.*

She recently told me, "It was really that simple; after that nothing was the same. I remember thinking I can just start tomorrow and choose to be happy and choose to try my absolute hardest in everything I do in that moment and see what happens. After we won NCAAs, I remember thinking, 'Oh my gosh, it happened!' "

We won the 2010 NCAA championship at the end of Anna's senior year, the year she started off by choosing happy. For Anna's first three years with us, she was extremely inconsistent with her beam series, a back handspring to a layout step out. She embodied the term "hit or miss." But what was so weird to me was that whenever one of her teammates was really struggling with that series Anna would be the one to coach her, telling her the exact technique needed to hit the series every time. So in September of her senior year, after she chose happy, I started coaching her up on her series and explained how well she fully understood the mechanics needed to be successful on that skill every single time. She agreed. So I suggested to her to get up on the beam and hit three series in a row. And she did it. I then told her to put those tallies up on the grease board and challenge herself to get to 10 by the end of the week. And she did. The 10th series was the most stressful, but she did it. Then she agreed to get to 20. By the end of her senior year she had not fallen on a beam series in training or competition and had hit 558 series in a row. She then went on to train to make the 2012 Olympic team and her streak continued. In the two years she trained elite, she hit another 1,392 series in a row!

At the warm-ups for the Olympic trials, I was sitting in the stands and I looked to my right where Anna was warming up on beam. She fell. I chuckled. And she chuckled. Someone very wise once said, "Streaks were made to be broken." At that point she had hit 1,950 beam series in a row. A far cry from the initial three she was not certain she could do. Anna hit the refresh button, trained for the Olympic Games, earned the alternate spot on the Olympic team, and retired without ever missing again. The mind is a very powerful thing.

It's super important to recognize that Anna didn't get more talented, stronger, or in better shape. Anna simply chose to think of the things that would make her successful versus all of the negative things she'd been used to telling herself.

Next time you have a choice to make, visualize the chain of events that might result from it; it may help you make your decision.

Chapter Fifteen

Intentional Movement

"Life is not a spectator sport."

—Jackie Robinson

There is a basic formula for crafting floor routines. Just like any other art form, the artist can craft something sound that works for the purpose of acquiring a good score; however, in anything crafted to capture someone else's attention, it's not the expected that is interesting—it's the unexpected. Because of my dance background (and my early ignorance of the rules and traditions of the sport) I have been known to craft innovative and unique floor routines that have set the UCLA program apart. I believe it's important to emphasize the *artistic* part of artistic gymnastics, not to just create routines to fulfill the scoring requirements. Even before everything was recorded, clipped, and posted online I had earned a reputation as a choreographer within the sport. I have no doubt had the internet existed in previous generations many more gymnasts would have gone viral (meaning over 4 million-ish views), such as the great Olga Korbut, who I believe was the first gymnast to truly capture the attention of people outside of the gymnastics universe. Now that social media has become a mass distribution channel, four routines—three from UCLA—have gone viral, including routines by Sophina De Jesus in 2016, which had over 50 million views in three days; Hallie Mossett in 2017, with, as of this writing, over 11 million views; and Katelyn Ohashi in 2018, again, as of this writing, with over 60 million views and counting. The only other collegiate gymnast (that I know of) to have a routine go viral is Lloimincia Hall from LSU with 5 million views. Our floor exercise videos going viral has become so common that in March of 2016 the *Los Angeles Times* interviewed me for a piece on that very topic, "Why UCLA gymnasts' videos keep going viral."

So why, indeed, these routines? I would imagine most hardcore gymnastics fans would not count these routines in their favorites because they deviate too much from the tradition of classic artistry and elegance associated with gymnastics. The point being, it takes a lot more viewers than just gymnastics fans to produce the numbers to qualify as "going viral."

I believe these routines went viral for a few reasons. First, each of these routines had music that was highly relatable to the average person, so the start of the routine immediately caught everyone's attention. Second, the choreography in all of these routines is, again, highly relatable. Gymnastics can be thought of as an "elite" or "high-brow" sport and all of these routines had choreography that anyone could do or at least relate to. Lloimincia Hall incorporated natural dance moves that brought her choice of highly popular gospel music to life. Sophina DeJesus's entire routine was one popular dance move after another, including the Whip, Nae Nae, and ubiquitous Dab. Hallie Mossett paid a tribute to Beyoncé, including parts from the infamous "Single Ladies" choreography. And Katelyn Ohashi was pure Michael Jackson. All of these routines get your own inner rhythm pumping regardless of how much of a curmudgeon you might be externally. And, third, every one of these routines conveyed pure joy to the audience. During Olga Korbut's Olympic gold medal floor routine from 1972, the announcer mentioned how she "beams from the floor and plays with the crowd with her eyes and her smile." Just as we love to watch videos of puppies, we love to watch other things that bring us happiness.

Last, in watching all of these routines again, I see that each of them has a signature, memorable move. I've always felt this was extremely important in choreography. I always want to leave the audience with a visual memory of the routine, which has to be a clean, clear picture they can remember. For Olga it was her middle pass, which was a laid out back flip landing in a chest roll. Lloimincia's is her infamous seat drop, perfectly placed at the most impactful transition of her music. Sophina's was when she got as close to the audience as she could, smiled and whipped and nae nae'd... at that moment you wanted to be her friend and go dancing with her. For Hallie it was halfway through her routine when the music changed to Beyoncé's "Single Ladies" and everyone got excited to do the famous choreography right along with her. And for Katelyn, it's right before her last pass when the music drops, she drops to her knee, and immediately the music picks up with a heavy down beat, which you can't help but clap along to, and... wait for it... she immediately does her last tumbling pass, which ends in a split drop to the floor immediately springing right back to her feet. It's the perfect exclamation point for an ending to whip the crowd into a frenzy!

Whether you like, love, hate, dislike, or are indifferent to these routines, one thing is indisputable: these athletes chose to venture outside the standard accepted formula for crafting a traditional floor routine, which is why they attracted worldwide attention. These athletes and many others like them who have the courage to dare to be different are one of the biggest reasons why our sport is exploding with global popularity.

It's massively fun to see the final product on the competition floor even though I find the process to be a struggle. For me, the fun part is getting the myriad of different reactions and comments to our new floor routines each year.

When I think about the things I love about being the head coach of the UCLA gymnastics team, they are the relationships with the student-athletes, coaching balance beam because it is such a mental event, and team meetings. Believe it or not my least favorite part of the process is actually crafting the routines. Shocking, I know! That goes for balance beam as well. And while I'm at it, let me repeat that I don't like giving pregame speeches.

With that said, I know exactly why I dislike choreographing floor and beam. First of all, the gymnastics code of points by which the athletes are judged dictates the elements that need to be included in routine compositions, and each routine must contain specific skills. When I very first started choreographing routines I would often, many times without realizing it, include beautiful but difficult movement that was worthless in the code of points—not a wise coaching tactic when judges are looking to deduct points for every misstep. By removing those beautiful elements and considering the length of routines can only be 1:30, it doesn't leave time to develop choreographic flow or storyline through the movement. I often feel I'm building on a particular pattern of dance and then I think, "Oh shoot, I still have to put in the leap pass and only have 15 seconds left of the routine."

The code of points also dictates what is considered a "skill." If it's not a skill, the judges can deduct for lack of execution. Years ago, I remember choreographing a two and a half turn in someone's floor routine in order to create a unique transition in the choreography. This was before the skill was in the code of points. It wasn't a double or a triple, and even though she executed it flawlessly, our athlete got a deduction because it wasn't in the code of points. Frustrating!

Then there was the time I specifically added a small leap where I *didn't* want the athlete to hit a 180 degree split; the leap was meant as a transition, a "breath" from one movement to the other. Nope. The judges deducted for not having enough amplitude or showing enough split.

Our sport is called *artistic* gymnastics, but sometimes it feels like the judges and the code of points only care or reward acrobatics, regardless of artistic intention.

And then there was the time Leah Homma used the song "Sadeness" by Enigma and the last eight counts of music in her routine were just breathing. Leah was a two-time Pac-10 Gymnast of the Year, helped us win our first national championship in 1997, is one of the greatest gymnasts in Canadian history, and was a gorgeous dancer with a light, ethereal yet mesmerizing quality. I thought the breathing was a beautiful way to decrescendo her routine to the final pose. One judge looked at me with a stoic look and said, "Nice routine, get rid of the sex scene at the end." Sex scene? It was breathing! But yes, I begrudgingly changed it.

Oh, and this really ticked me off. Many times choreographers will repeat movement to lend a choreographic memorable moment. I chose to do this with a particular phrase of music in Kiralee Hayashi's floor routine. The music repeated for two eight counts so I had Kiralee repeat the choreography. After the meet the judge said to me, "Really, you couldn't come up with something different so you had to repeat?" When I got home that night I pulled up some of my most favorite masterpieces of George Balanchine, choreographic genius of the New York City Ballet, and proved (at least to myself) that I wasn't lazy or incompetent and that repetitive movement can be very powerful.

Hang on, I'm not done. Another pet peeve of mine on floor is that *most* gymnasts' choreography can only be composed turning in toward the standing leg instead of away from it. The reason most gymnasts can't execute turns turning "outside" or away is because their baby toes get caught in the floor carpet, which opens the door to stumbling, spraining their foot, or breaking a toe. Some choose to wear a rhythmic gymnastics shoe on one or both feet, but most gymnasts don't like the feel of them when they're tumbling. As someone who grew up as a dancer and dance choreographer (not a gymnastics choreographer) it feels rather monotonous to be so limited in ways of getting the body to twist and turn on the floor. When I get to choreograph for dancers on a dance floor it feels like my whole body and mind are free to interpret the movement. When choreographing on a gymnastics floor I feel like a part of the choreographic stimulus is stifled because of carpet issues.

My final salvo for why I don't really enjoy choreographing floor routines is because, as I've realized, it all comes down to "being judged." In my opinion, Angi Cipra, 2017 All-American on floor, is inarguably one of the best floor performers who has ever done gymnastics. She understood that her face is part of her body, which in turn means that when I choreographed her facial expressions there was intention behind them. When she competed she came to life and would draw everyone in the audience into her floor experience.

After one exceptional routine where I, her teammates, and the other coaches all *knew* she was going to receive a 10, one judge gave her a 10, but the other gave her a 9.95 claiming that while she had great facial expression toward the audience, she "didn't direct her attention to *him*" and that was the reason for his 0.05 deduction. WHAT?! Facial expressions aren't even discussed in the code of points. It's simply something our team does because the face is part of the body; therefore, I choreograph the whole body. And this is what it feels like to be in a subjective sport! Yes, it's just a score, but Angi missed out on getting into the illustrious perfect 10 history books because one judge reserved the right to be, well, judgmental.

Again, I have a reputation as being a rather good choreographer. My point in mentioning all of this is that you don't have to love every part of your job to excel at it. Even though there are all of these reasons why I don't love this part of my job, I do approach each routine with purposeful enthusiasm. I look at it as a new challenge to craft something interesting, entertaining, and possibly iconic.

I purposefully refrain from ever using the word "create" when expressing my craft. I follow Balanchine in this. He would use the term "craftsman" when speaking of himself as a choreographer. He was quoted as saying "God creates. Woman inspires. And man assembles." When I first started choreographing I restructured this per my own philosophies and came up with "God creates. Music Inspires. And woman assembles."

So, how *do* I choreograph? I'm often asked about this. I hear the music and then I see pictures in my head of the movement. When I'm choreographing for gymnasts there are always a few things I make sure they understand. First, unless specifically choreographed otherwise, *all* arm movements start with the elbow. That prevents the movement from looking stiff, and infuses life into the movements. Think about it, most natural arm movement starts from the elbow. Imagine throwing a ball without using your elbow. I always joke with our athletes, "God gave you an elbow for a reason. USE IT!"

Second, there is the importance of *transitions*. There are a lot of gymnasts who are good "posers," but there is no life in their performances because they don't understand the importance of getting from one pose to the other...the *transition*!

Third, the face is part of the body! And the eyes are part of the face. I spend as much time choreographing the eyes of an athlete as I do the rest of her body.

The last thing I always discuss with a gymnast when I'm first starting to choreograph a routine is that there are "two fronts." In dance, there is usually a single defined "front" where the audience sits. In gymnastics there is seating on all four sides of the floor. However, in most gymnastics arena setups, there are only "two fronts" where the majority of the audience is seated—the other sides have the uneven parallel bars apparatus on one side and the balance beam on the other. How choreography is staged to take into consideration the two fronts makes a huge difference in how a floor routine is viewed and received by the audience and consequently by the judges.

To improve everyone's whole-body movement and to loosen them up, one of the really fun things I do is to have them take all different types of dance classes. Classical, salsa, hip-hop, anything to help them face any awkwardness they might feel and expose them to new movements and rhythms. I've even had a burlesque instructor come to the gym and teach new movements. For that class I turned off the lights and left the room so they could explore without feeling judged. I loved this because the instructor focused on teaching sensual movement without being bump-and-grind trashy.

I've even had dancers and choreographers, including gymnastics icon Cathy Rigby who went on to play Peter Pan on Broadway, talk to our team about how to audition. She talked to them about how to show up dressed, how to act, how much makeup to wear, how and when to introduce themselves to the production team, and most importantly, the importance of establishing personal parameters before the audition starts.

A dear friend of mine, Ferly Prado, has a prolific dance résumé, which includes being a lead dancer for Tina Turner, Britney Spears, Justin Timberlake, Beyoncé, and Cher. I often ask her to talk to our athletes. Ferly is tall, blond, and *gorgeous*, and she has enjoyed a great career as a dancer while maintaining her dignity and moral compass. She talks straight with our team and says, "I don't care how great the part is, I don't do nudity of any kind. As soon as I'm asked to remove my top I graciously say, 'Thank you—this part isn't for me,' and I leave the audition." Ferly shattered any preconceived notions about a sexy, tall, blond Vegas dancer and, most importantly, Ferly modeled for our team what it looks like to own your choices.

The most impactful lesson I offer our athletes to help expand their movement quality is an acting 101 class. It takes place every time they do their floor routine. Since I first started working with gymnasts I have choreographed each of their floor routines in line with a particular character. Brittani McCullough's 2010 national championship routine was infused with African worship dance from her church and her character was a beautiful African warrior princess. Angi Cipra was a 12-year-old tomboy who followed her big sister into a dance club and found her nirvana. Anna Li's iconic senior routine told the story of her life in gymnastics, through pain and heartache to finding her voice, her strength, and ultimately, her joy.

I started using this acting technique within their floor routines to improve their movement quality and to give their movement meaning—to make it much more interesting to watch. By the time the gymnasts perform in competition I want their performances to be captivating. I tell them that right after they salute the judge and before they walk on the competition floor exercise mat, they are in character. Just like any great stage performer, you stay in character for the entire time you're on that stage. They can break character when they are off the floor and have assimilated back into the team.

Dressing up as their characters has enhanced their story-telling; it's something we call "Operation Peacock," an idea first implemented by two team members, Anna Li and Vanessa "Zam" Zamarripa. Listen to interviews from your favorite actor and they'll comment on how their character really came to life when they got in makeup and put on the costume.

Anna recalls when she and Zam first suggested the idea. We were going to have a floor intra-squad on a Saturday, so a few days before she talked to the team. "Miss Val keeps trying to get us to bring out the choreography through our characters," she said. "So let's dress up in our characters to help bring our floor routines to life." They called it an obscure name to keep it secret from us coaches. We came in for training that day and they were all in these crazy costumes. We coaches looked at each other dumbfounded and asked, "Okay... what's up?" And then they started performing their floor dance-throughs *in character*. It was a magical transformation. They finally were embodying the movements with emotion, something most gymnasts don't ever do.

The part that stood out the most for me was how every one of them came to life in their faces, whether they were cold-blooded assassins, African queens of the desert, reptiles, or in Anna's case, telling the painful yet exuberant story of her life. They finally knew what it felt like to give themselves permission and the freedom to *perform*.

Like floor, when it comes to choreographing beam routines I have issues there too. I believe the hardest event in gymnastics is the balance beam. Think about this: you're ready to compete, you have adrenaline pumping throughout your body, and then you have to focus and channel it all onto a four-inch-wide platform. This does not lend itself to what is natural in athletics. Athletics is about preparing well, getting in the zone, and going for it. With beam you have to learn to silence everything around you and focus your energy onto those four inches without holding back. As soon as you hold back to try and stay on the beam, you will fall off. You have to be this perfect combination of aggression, calmness, and confidence. I think balance beam is a master class in emotional control.

It's also the event that most translates to life. As we mature and realize we are accountable for our words and actions, we learn the art of communication. More often than not we are most successful when we communicate passionately and confidently yet with focus, with purpose, and calm confidence.

I find crafting beam routines to be stifling because they are two-dimensional. All of the movement goes forward or backward. Traditionally, it's a lot of posing. I guess I could look at this as a challenge, but I honestly don't enjoy it. I think it's also difficult for me to come up with interesting movement on beam because there is no music, therefore no motivation for the movement. I do have the athletes practice "dance-throughs" to their own music to develop a consistent rhythm for their routines. A cue I often tell them before they compete is "Kick in your rhythm."

All that said, balance beam is often thought of as the make-or-break event, which makes it extremely important to have an immensely confident leadoff competitor. The first up on beam usually isn't your superstar or most flashy athlete but someone who is consistent and reliable and who can set a confident pulse for the rest of the lineup to build on.

As a senior Anna Li was one of our best beam workers—and she was definitely flashy. She had earned one of the prestigious competitive spots at the end of the lineup where the scores are commonly more favorable. Early on in the competitive season she told me that she wanted to take over the leadoff spot on beam. Anna explained she knew she could compete week after week with the confidence her team would need to infuse all of them with the same confidence. It worked! She worked on beam like it was her playground.

At the 2010 national championships we had competed the first half of the meet well, but not stellar. During a bye round we headed to the locker room. It was just our first year working with Foster Mobley, but I greatly valued his opinion. I invited him to come down to the locker room in the middle of the championships. He waited as we gathered our thoughts and then leaned over to me and said, "Miss Val, do you mind if I say something to the girls?"

I instinctively trusted him and said, "I don't mind at all, go for it," not knowing what he was going to say.

Foster commented that the essence of this team was fun, happy, tight together, collaborative. A band of sisters—that was their character. What he saw in the first two rounds was not that. They were tight and were performing away from their character.

Going into beam the team committed to loosening up and enjoying the experience more, knowing if we went into beam tight it would be a disaster. Anna led us off in a fashion that was more than even I would have asked for. Three-quarters of the way through her routine she ad-libbed a fun dance move to the music that was playing in the arena and smiled at her teammates before drilling her dismount. Her teammates went crazy. It was the perfect amount of sass and fun they needed to follow her lead. We nailed every beam routine after that, went to floor, and won the NCAA championship before our last performer ever went.

While there's no way I could have known this, Foster emphasized to my coauthor, Coop, "No other coach would have allowed me to talk to their athletes in the middle of the National Championship event with a message that had not been screened by them first, or at all; and if it did get that far it would have been delivered by the coach."

Bravo to all of you who dare to do you. You not only help make our world more exciting and colorful but you also set an example for those who are still fearful of stepping out of accepted norms and into the unknown and often scary world of being different!

Chapter Sixteen

Owning Your Stage

"Art is the only way to run away without leaving home."

—Twyla Tharp

Now that I've sufficiently whined about what I don't like about crafting floor routines and the thought process of what goes in to making them work, let me share some of my favorite and most memorable moments. My all-time favorite beginning move of a floor routine was in 1983 for Donna Kemp, an amazing gymnast who later won the American Athletic Inc. Award given to the nation's top senior gymnast. The music started and she immediately wound up and executed a spot-on triple turn. BAM! It got everyone's attention, it was exciting, and she hit it every time. Innovation proved magical.

Another breathtaking moment came in the middle of Kim Hamilton's floor routines where she did a simple roundoff layout step out. The awe came from the fact she was five feet seven and had gorgeous long legs that seemed to float forever as we all waited for her to land back on the ground. *This was a perfect example of the awesomeness of simplicity.* She embodied one of my favorite quotes, "Simplicity is the ultimate sophistication."

And still, one of my all-time favorite finishes was the last eight counts of Leah Homma's routine to just breathing, a.k.a., "the sex scene."

So what floor routines are my favorites? That is an *impossible* question to answer. There are so many because each of our athletes is unique and brings her own style and interpretive dynamics to the choreography. While I can't begin to enumerate my favorites, I can share the routines that I thought pushed the artistic envelope and furthered the artistic quality of the sport.

When Kim Hamilton entered the gym the first time back in 1986, I was still an assistant coach. I had never seen a gymnast that tall before. I turned to Jerry, the head coach, and asked, "Why are you recruiting a track girl?" Kim's tall frame and legs were gorgeous, I often referred to Kim as a thoroughbred. By embracing the uniqueness of her physical frame, the result was stunning gymnastics. Just as Misty Copeland changed the definition of what a typical ballerina can look like, Kim changed perceptions of what a gymnast can look like— there's never been another gymnast with her stature, ability, musculature, and artistry. Kim became a three-time NCAA floor champion.

Tanya Service, now Tanya Chaplin and Oregon State head coach, was on the same team as Kim. Tanya was extremely "quick twitch." This ability aided her to move beautifully and effortlessly through intricate turning choreography (without catching her baby toes). She was so quick twitch that to this day she is the only gymnast I know of who did a cartwheel double back dismount off the beam. Gym nerds, yes, you read that correctly. It was a *cartwheel double back*, not a *roundoff*.

Heidi Moneymaker, UCLA gymnast and two-time NCAA champion, was super fun to work with because she would try anything. The crazier, the better. All of her floor routines were exceptionally unique, fast twitch, and crazy dance. To this day I can remember how much fun I had working with Heidi, not because she was the best dancer, but because she tried anything and everything and *never* worried that she might look silly. *Ever.* No wonder she became one of the top stunt artists in Hollywood. Heidi has nearly 100 stunt credits to her name, including being a double for Scarlett Johansson as Black Widow in the Marvel Avenger movies and Michelle Rodriguez in *Fast & Furious*. She has also made appearances in other major blockbusters from *Rambo* to *Star Trek*.

Stella Umeh is inarguably one of the most artistic gymnasts in the world. Her understanding of movement quality and musicality was unmatched, which lent itself nicely to a long career with *Cirque du Soleil* once she graduated from UCLA.

Amy Thorne pulled off a satirical routine like an Academy Award– winning actress. Amy was a non-scholarship athlete "walk-on" who earned UCLA's first ever perfect 10! Anyone who has worked in the entertainment industry knows how hard it is to pull off satire. It's very easy to overdo and look contrived. Amy's performance was brilliant.

Anna Li is forever on my list for boldly embracing that dramatic minute and a half floor routine that told her story of despair, distrust, and insecurity and to instead take charge of her life, choose happy, and find joy.

Elyse Hopfner-Hibbs is simply an amazing dancer. Elyse not only moved fast and seductively at the same time, but she was also a master at penetrating one's soul with her piercing blue eyes. She was an equally brilliant performer on balance beam as well.

Brittani McCullough mastered the art of the catwalk on the gymnastics floor. Captivating the audience with powerful tumbling, dramatic dance, and the catwalk—literally walking around the floor for a full eight counts staring down the audience. She was the quintessential student-athlete; she won the NCAA floor title in 2010 while she was in nursing school, posting 36 hours a week of clinical rotations in a neonatal intensive care unit.

Ariana Berlin dared to blend the street genres of hip-hop and break-dancing into the world of artistic gymnastics and did it beautifully. She's the only gymnast I know of who freestyled in break-dancing fashion the last 16 counts of her floor routine, bringing the house down every time, even at away meets.

Hallie Mossett absolutely commanded the arena with a simple tilt of her head and the snap of her fingers. She learned how to pay homage to her favorite performer Beyoncé while finding her own unique style and movement quality to stamp on her routine.

Angi Cipra was probably the best actor/performer I've ever worked with. Angi understood how the subtlety of a facial expression could transcend choreography and bring a performance to life. Angi is currently a performer in *Le Rêve* at Wynn, Las Vegas.

One of my greatest heartbreaks is that I never got to choreograph a college floor routine for Christine "Peng-Peng" Lee. Peng arrived at UCLA with a horrific knee injury that forced her to miss two seasons of competition, but that also allowed her to stay in our program for six years. While she was never able to compete more than bars and beam for us, on those apparatuses, Peng has a way of bringing movement to life unlike any other gymnast on the planet.

As of this writing, Gracie Kramer is our latest most impressive artist. She plays an alien trying to break out of a mental institution! Her timing and ability to bring music to life through movement is remarkable and not something one can easily teach.

And then there's Felicia Hano; Katelyn Ohashi, 2018 reigning floor exercise champion; Danusia Francis; Sophina DeJesus; and… I could go on for pages. This is where I probably will hurt a lot of feelings for not including everyone. The truth is I really have been blessed with so much amazing talent to work with all these years. So let me just say it: if you see your name here or not, you are *all* remarkable artists in so many ways!

Now, choreographing for SeaWorld's summer Cirque-style attractions is a very different experience, but with its own unique rewards. Each year we hire about 30 performers, a third of whom are "newbies"; they have never performed or had formal gymnastics, dance, or acrobatic training. I have to admit, I have a blast coaching them up like they're

Olympic athletes. I am relentless with everything: technique, form, movement quality, musicality, counting music, facial expressions, the importance of transitions, and the appropriate demeanor in rehearsal. For them to tell me from across the stage, "Miss Val, I'm just really tired," is probably not the best choice, but yes, it has happened numerous times.

For those newbies, I have to start from scratch with the rules of theatre, reiterating, "If you can see the audience the audience can see you." This concept is also a simple fact of life. Any time you are in public someone is watching you.

The rules of theatre include backstage performance etiquette as well; "No, it's not okay to burp and fart in the dressing room filled with other male and female performers." Yes, I actually had to give this talk recently. It also included, "I'm not interested in your personal hygiene philosophy; use deodorant."

While I can't believe how many times I have to repeat "straighten your legs," "point your feet," and "stand up on 1, not 1 and…" it is their onstage dynamic showmanship that is the biggest challenge. Most of them bring it sporadically throughout the number, but they don't understand how to keep that taut-inner-pulsing-magical-hum throughout the whole show.

Last summer I was about to give my last "pregame" speech to the cast before our show opened when I had a revelation: tell them to tap into their inner Rock Star!

When was the last time you saw a timid or cautious rock star? When have you ever seen a rock star crumble in humiliation and embarrassment when they made a mistake? When have you ever seen a rock star not have a certifiable strut—admittedly some may seem awkward, but regardless, they *own it*! Think Mick Jagger—now that's a strut.

So how do I get newbies to tap into their inner rock stars? They have to realize that everything they do is part of the show; they need to execute their performance with confidence and if they happen to make a mistake, then they need to continue with conviction. The only time I ever received a standing ovation during my dance career was when I made a massive mistake. I was performing a solo where I was doing step, high kick, step, high kick—en pointe. On one of the kicks, my pointe shoe came out from underneath me and I flew up and landed smack on my tailbone, which I couldn't get up quickly from. Everybody in the theatre gasped. I got up, I smiled, did a little curtsy, and I finished the number. The audience saw a moment of authenticity, humanism, and earned humility. I was real onstage and I was rewarded for it. There is no failure (remember I don't believe in the F-word), just the exciting and often unpredictable nature of live performance.

To be a rock star you need to own the skills, style, and flair you bring to your daily life. A great example of this has do with floor sensation Hallie Mossett. Before the 2016–2017 season I was advising Hallie on her choreography. She was working to emulate Queen Bey herself, Beyoncé. I thought it was a little too on the nose. I told her, "Hallie, don't be a second-rate Beyoncé, be a first-rate you." She accepted my suggestion and honored Beyoncé's moves and then worked in her own choreography and became a viral internet sensation—getting picked up by *Time, US Weekly, Cosmopolitan*, and many others. She created something new and unique and *that's* a gift to the world! Hallie didn't turn into Beyoncé; she performed some of her hit moves with her own flair and established her own following.

Rock stars know people pay to see them perform. The attendees are fans who want to say they just witnessed a great performance. Rock stars don't go onstage wondering if the crowd will like them; they understand the audience has already purchased their tickets.

This is the same for gymnasts, SeaWorld performers, and *you*, whether you're on a stage or behind a desk. Your employer hired *you*! They bought a ticket to see *you* perform. Execute your job with confidence. News flash: your boyfriend, girlfriend, or spouse bought a ticket, too! They are on your side and want you to succeed. So, create, cultivate, and own your personal cadence, your inner swagger with an unapologetic, strong magical hum. Embrace and present your inner rock star to the world!

Chapter Seventeen

What Success Really Looks Like

"Success is peace of mind, which is a direct result in knowing you've done your best."

—JOHN WOODEN

What we consider traditional is what we have chosen to honor and normalize. This becomes culture. *When you put winning above people you open up your organization to a corrosiveness that can spread like cancer.* However, we can choose to be different. We can choose gratitude, curiosity, openness, diversity, and joy. We can choose to put the health and well-being of those around us as our driving force. This is how we can all motivate change.

There are a few life-coaching clichés I don't agree with and feel do more harm than their intended good. One is that we should strive for "perfection." Perfection doesn't exist, which is why when you strive to be perfect it's easy to give up before you've even begun. After all, why expend the energy if you know you'll never make the goal. It's a sentiment that's twice as hard when you're uninspired to tackle a particular thing. Instead, within our program we strive for excellence. Hard. Stratospheric. But always achievable.

The other idiom I'm not a fan of is "I'm going to give 150 percent." That's fantasy. Effort doesn't exist over 100 percent. As soon as someone says, "Miss Val, I'm going to give you 150 percent on this next turn," I say, "Cut the crap and dramatic effect, aim for 100 percent and you and I both will be thrilled with your effort and quite possibly the result."

The philosophy I do embrace is *getting 1 percent better.* Every day at the beginning of training we discuss the plan for the day and then discuss what 1 percent better will look like for them as individuals and as a team. Imagine an athlete one day getting 1 percent better in technique, form, and mental discipline. Then getting 1 percent better in technique, form, and discipline the next day. And the next day. Wow! The compounding effect of such incremental improvement would reach near-superhero status, but it is also absolutely achievable. The one Bruin who immediately comes to mind when I think of getting 1 percent better is Sadiqua Bynum. She has often talked about how much that concept really helped her. I asked her to explain and she told me the following:

I remember when it hit me that I can change each day and make that day better by doing one little thing different. It's easy to go through the day and not think about how that day is going to turn out, but if you think about getting 1 percent better you can make a change. When I was in high school, they tried to inspire me by saying "Perfect practice makes perfect." That never helped me because it made me feel like if it wasn't perfect, I was failing. When I came to college I was a lot harder on myself than I should have been because that phrase was on my mind. Embracing the concept of 1 percent better was when my gymnastics got better a lot faster. One percent better is up to me. I liked the fact I could determine what 1 percent better meant for me that day. Whether it was my form or becoming more efficient in my training, pointing my toes more or taking turns faster. If I did it more efficiently it was 1 percent better, even if it wasn't perfect, I knew I was getting better. It became even more important for me to embrace this concept in my junior year of college, the year my brother passed. It really hit me that each day isn't promised, if I could get 1 percent better each day, then it will make each last day just that much more meaningful.

I've coached seven NCAA championship teams. All of those trophies are somewhere in our athletic department. The only trophy I have in my office is our fourth place finish from 2007.

We went into the first round of that championship meet tied for eighth, praying for a miracle that everything would come together and we'd make it to the next and final round, the Super Six. We did!

But our team was decimated with injuries and the athletes who were able to compete were also banged up, and many of them hadn't been able to train much before the championship.

The night before the Super Six, we coaches got together and decided to go for broke. We chose to put in a lineup of our highest *potential* scores versus the athletes we knew would hit. I'll forever remember the gleam in the eyes of the athletes when we told them the plan. I looked at Jordan Schwikert (sister to Tasha Schwikert and just as immensely gifted and talented) and Ariana Berlin, both of whom hadn't trained floor in over four weeks because of nagging injuries and asked them if they could get through a floor routine. Both Jordan and Ariana looked at me like gladiators being called into battle and embraced the opportunity. We made similar adjustments in our lineup on all four events, choosing to compete athletes who, *if* they hit their *best* routine, would outscore the athlete they were replacing by a quarter or half a 10th.

I was betting on gymnasts who may or may not have been able to actually do a full gymnastics routine. I told them, "If halfway through your routine you know you don't have the gas for your last tumbling pass, then dummy it down and make sure to finish safely." The coaching staff and I were definitely leaping in with uncertainty. It was exhilarating. However, the most important part of the discussion was when each athlete looked me in the eye and said, "I can do this." With all the uncertainty on the table that bond of trust is something they still talk about over a decade later.

That was one of the most exhilarating competitions I've ever coached. Every single one of our athletes performed their personal best. As athletes and as a team we reached the top of Coach Wooden's Pyramid of Success: competitive greatness; we were able to bring our best when our best was needed. We finished fourth, four places higher than we had reached all season.

I feel I've always been a grateful person. Throughout my life I've felt a sense of luck and appreciation for my circumstances. To be a woman during this time, in this country, in this city has provided me with innumerable *unearned* opportunities I can't begin to appreciate enough.

At no point in my life has this been more evident than September 11, 2001. It was 7:00 a.m. and I was driving to UCLA for the first day of our 2001–2002 season. Bobby was on his way to the campus as well when he pulled up next to me at a stop light and told me to turn on the radio. From the stereo speakers I heard the horrific news of two planes flying into the World Trade Center buildings. Shock. Numb. Outrage.

At 8:00 a.m. I was scheduled to welcome our new team and discuss what it means to be a UCLA Bruin, the plan for the season, and the schedule of meetings and strength tests for that initial week. Obviously, all of that was no longer relevant and I had exactly 30 minutes to come up with something meaningful and poignant to address our student-athletes in the most horrific time that any of us had ever experienced.

Having absolutely no idea what I should say, I called Coach Wooden for advice. I didn't realize it at the time, but coach had implemented the Broken Record technique on me while I was executing the Ask, the Nudge, and the Drop.

The conversation went something like this:

"Coach, I'm sickened by the news and at a total loss for what to say to our team, whom I'm meeting with in 20 minutes."

"It is indeed horrible what has happened. Don't worry, Honey. Just listen to your heart, you'll know what to say."

"Uhhhhhhhh, Coach. Can you give me at least a little idea of what to say? I've got nothing!"

"Don't worry, Honey. Just trust and follow your heart."

Starting to panic, wanting/needing to have the perfect words of leadership to comfort our young student-athletes I was at a total loss, "Okay, thank you, Coach. I love you."

Nothing. I had nothing.

Amidst the emotions I had swirling inside me was also a deep concern for Kristen Maloney (part of the 2000 Olympic team with fellow Bruin teammates Jamie Dantzscher, Tasha Schwikert, and Alyssa Beckerman) who was scheduled to fly to LA the night before from Pennsylvania. News reports had confirmed a plane in Pennsylvania had been hijacked and gone down. I had yet to hear if Kristen had made it to campus.

It's now 8:00 a.m. and we start our first team meeting of the season. The student-athletes file into the meeting room. Somber. Tearful.

Uncertain. Shocked. My heart leapt when I saw Kristen was among them. At that point rumors had started circulating that it was a terrorist attack.

I asked our team how they were feeling. There wasn't a lot of talk. A few started to utter broken sentences of confusion. Questions were swirling of what exactly had happened. Mostly they were in shock. Then Carly Raab, one of our student-athletes spoke up and said, "Miss Val, what has just happened in New York is the worst thing I've ever experienced and I'm all the way across the country in California. I can't imagine going into the gym and doing gymnastics. I want to get on a plane and go help out anyway I can. Why would we ever do gymnastics again?"

And then it hit me. The clarity Coach Wooden told me I'd have. The answer to Carly's question was crystal clear ... *because we can:*

Because we live in a country that provides us the freedom as women to do sports.

Why should we go in the gym and train gymnastics?... Because we can.

And when we do, and every day forward we will do gymnastics with more appreciation and intention to be our best as our way of saying "thank you" to those who fought for this freedom. Because we can.

Coach Wooden was known to never give advice—he never felt it was his place. As much as I wanted him to tell me exactly what to say to our team on that fateful morning, he actually gave me the greatest advice I could have received, "Trust and follow your heart." What I said to our team was raw and heartfelt, and it addressed the concerns of our athletes versus a prefabricated speech of what I would have anticipated they needed to hear.

Coach Wooden, like life, didn't give me what I asked for—he gave me what I needed. Thank you, Coach.

Chapter Eighteen

The Importance of Attention to Intention

"It is often in the darkest skies that we see the brightest stars."

—RICHARD EVANS

The trampoline metaphor is one of my most favorite visuals for team building. It focuses on the importance of supporting each other and holding each other accountable. The purpose of a trampoline bed is to withstand pressure. The tighter the trampoline threads are woven, the more pressure the trampoline can handle.

I start out with the team each year by waving my fingers in the air and saying, "Each finger represents a trampoline thread, and each thread represents one of you, our coaches, and staff. Right now our team is like this..." and I loosely weave my fingers together. "Our goal in these next three months before season starts is to get like this…" and I lace my fingers tightly together. "The tighter the bond, the more adversity and pressure we as a team will be able to handle, just like a trampoline bed. So what happens if one of these threads gets frayed? That area becomes the most vulnerable part of the trampoline bed. If that thread doesn't get the care it needs to get stitched up strong again, eventually the trampoline bed will break through at that point and it will no longer serve its purpose in being able to handle pressure. We need to take care to keep each other strong and healthy. Through that care for each other we will be more tightly bonded and the more adversity we will be able to handle."

I had absolutely no idea just how important these words—and so many of my other philosophies—would become to my life outside the gym.

It was the spring of 2014 and I was driving home after a day of errands. My phone rang and I picked it up. It was my doctor. She told me to pull the car over to the side of the road. She said, "Your tests have come back positive. You have breast cancer."

My world went silent.

My mind immediately went to the horrific experiences my mother, Rosie, had gone through 30 years earlier with colon cancer, which eventually resulted in a very debilitating, slow, painful, and dehumanizing death. There was no history of breast cancer on either side of my family, though. Just one week earlier, I had done a breast self-examination because I had been experiencing pain in my left breast. Oddly, I felt a hard something in my right breast; it felt like a pulled muscle, not like the pea-shaped lump you are told to look for.

On June 9th I went in to see my doctor who ordered a mammogram, then an ultrasound, and then a biopsy. On June 14th I got the call. That's the day my world stopped.

Even though I didn't know it at the time, this was about to become a crucible of everything I've been preaching throughout this book, my career, and life: making Choices, Owning my life, Attention to Intention, feeding my Thought Bubble , Act As If, the Ask, strengthening the Trampoline of people around me, the importance of Presentation, finding the right Cue, and on and on.

While picking up the phone can be the first step toward changing your life, more often than not it's what you do after you hang up that requires even greater inner strength.

I hung up the phone and at that moment I heard a voice from the universe—God—say, *"Be anxious for nothing and grateful for all things."*

"What?" I thought. All noise around me had gone silent except for this voice telling me, *"Be anxious for nothing and grateful for all things."*

"Uhhh…God…I don't know if you heard, but I have CANCER!"

I heard it again. *"Be anxious for nothing and grateful for all things."*

I heard it as a shot of electric *gnosis*, a knowing. This sentence rattled around in my head as I tried to wrap my brain around the new information from my doctor.

I went home and told Bobby everything, including what I had heard repeatedly after I hung up the phone. First, he comforted me about my diagnosis. Then he said, "It's in the Bible. Be anxious for nothing…."

Sure, I had read parts of the Bible before, but I had never *thoroughly* read it. I went over and picked up the Bible, turned to Philippians 4:6–8, and there it was:

> Be anxious for nothing, but in every situation, by prayer and petition, with thanksgiving, present your requests to God. And the peace of God, which transcends all understanding, will guard your hearts and your minds in Christ Jesus.

OMG! Literally, oh my God. I *heard* this before I ever read it. This was a commandment not a suggestion.

The language in the Bible was a bit wordier than the message I heard, but maybe in God's great wisdom He knew it needed to be phrased in a simple manner I'd understand. After all, that's just good coaching—you have not taught until they have learned.

Be anxious for nothing! My life has been forever changed!

Rather than being engulfed in the fear and darkness of cancer, I was being commanded to not be anxious or fearful and instead to choose gratitude. But I didn't know how I was supposed to do this.

A few days after my biopsy I met with my oncologist who actually had a smile on her face as she described my breast cancer. She explained that I had stage 1 HER2-positive breast cancer. It was a very aggressive type of cancer; therefore I should begin treatments immediately. She said, "If you *choose* to, you're going to go through a year of chemo and surgery, but you'll be fine." I asked her how did she know this? She explained that I had gone from having the "worst" type of breast cancer to the "best." Had I been diagnosed just 10 years earlier there was no treatment for my specific type of cancer. Now, they knew the exact chemo cocktail that would work.

Be anxious for nothing.

At that moment I got it. I knew exactly how I wasn't going to be anxious. I understood the proverbial equation. The way to *not* be anxious was by living each moment in *gratitude*. I realized that anxiety and gratitude can't coexist in the brain. That being the case, I had to choose... I chose gratitude.

I don't *have to* get chemotherapy. I *get to* have chemo. It was a choice. My choice.

I knew I didn't want my cancer diagnosis to define who I was. Instead, with the endorsement of this positive news, I chose to embrace gratitude.

I get to have chemo. I *get* to have poison shot through my veins. And then I *get* to have surgery. I *get* to do all of these things that will hopefully give me more days. I *get* to breathe. I *get* to work. I *get* to dance. I *get* to hug my girls, and my family, and my grandchildren, and strangers! I *get* to put gas in my car because, yay, I have a car to put gas in. I *get* to wake up early to prepare for work because, yay, I have a job.

Do I like to get up early? No! Do I enjoy putting gas in my car? NO! But I get to because I can afford a car and I can afford the gas to put into the car. Am I looking forward to chemotherapy sessions?

Uh, that would be another "No." But this one revelation, "I *get to* ..." changed my outlook on everything I think about and do every day. I discovered an invaluable new cue to my life.

When I acknowledge that everything I do in life is a choice, I realize that the best decision I can make in any situation begins with gratitude. Gratitude is 100 percent choice. Gratitude isn't something I hope I could have, it's a deliberate effort in how I feel. I knew the choices I made the year of my cancer treatment would shape not only the recovery process but most likely my entire life. I told myself that difficulty and pain didn't have to stop me from *living*. I repeated it until I believed it and lived it. I didn't wait to get through chemotherapy so I could get on with my life, this was my life. Cancer was the spark that helped me refocus my daily choices.

The first step was to eliminate worry...be anxious for nothing. Actually, a few times that year I tried to prove God wrong, that there are, in fact, incidents where one should be anxious. As of this writing I still haven't found one.

Step two, "Be grateful for *all* things." Every. Little. Thing. When I go through my day being grateful for every single little thing, it doesn't leave time for complaining, negativity, or pity parties. Even though I went through a year of chemotherapy, double mastectomy, and four surgeries, I was more joyful and lived a more full life that year than any of my previous 56. One of our coaches and one of my dearest friends Randy Lane, whom I have known for over 25 years, recently told me the year I was dealing with cancer was the most relaxed he's ever seen me. Instead of succumbing to another midlife crisis, I decided—perhaps because of my cancer diagnosis—to have a "midlife awakening" and it has been amazing!

The first test of this philosophy happened during my initial visit with the oncologist. I learned there was a study for my type of cancer that was in its last phase of experimentation in which I could volunteer to potentially participate. There were two groups in the study. The first group was receiving traditional chemo. If I were in this group, I ran the risk of my hair falling out and feeling sick a lot of the time. The second group was receiving an experimental and very targeted treatment. It would attack only my malignant tumor, and as a result, my hair wouldn't fall out and I wouldn't feel very sick.

Yeah, I want to be in the second group! But my doctor informed me that it was a random draw. There was no avenue to take that would guarantee I would get "chosen" for the study.

"Does it help that I'm the head coach of the UCLA women's gymnastics team? And, I know the CEO of the UCLA hospital!"

The doctor replied, "You could know the president of the United States, it's not going to change the random selection for the study."

"Okay, how much does it cost then?" I tried.

"No, it's a study…a pure random draw," she tried to make me understand.

So, I was prepared to lose my hair and buy wigs or scarves. I was trying to consider what would make the team and my fellow coaches most comfortable when I was in the gym. Then, the day before I was due to start traditional chemotherapy, I found out that I had been randomly selected to be in the second group and receive the targeted experimental treatments! It was the only time during the entire process that I cried. I cried from sheer gratitude.

Be grateful for all things.

After being encouraged by my prognosis, I remember sitting on my couch in the sunlight and thinking about my situation and I began to fill up with gratitude at how fortunate my circumstances were. For the first time in my life that I can remember, I *exhaled*. This sounds trite, but let me assure you that it was one of the most memorable and powerful moments of my life. I literally, purposefully, gleefully *exhaled*. With that *exhale* came the life-altering *inhale*. A profound sense of my good fortune slowly hit after I inhaled while sitting on my couch, and I started chanting and eventually dancing, "I *get* to live, I GET to live, I GET to LIVE, I GET TO LIVE!"

At that moment I had another realization: we *all* have an expiration date; we just don't know when it is. At that moment I got infused with a zest for living that I'd never had before. I have always been an upbeat, positive, grateful person, but I was now feeling the inner excitement and drive that comes with not wanting to waste a single day. From that moment on, I've tried to live each moment of each day with as much purpose and intentional gratitude and fun as is humanly possible.

Everything I have done following my Great Exhale and resurrecting inhale has been purposeful. I purposefully referenced going to chemotherapy as going to my "Chemo Spa." A spa is where you go to get healthier. Sometimes even a traditional spa visit is painful—for any of you who have had a deep tissue massage or Rolfing, or even when the esthetician "extricates your pores" during a facial, you know it's not the most pleasant experience. Once you reframe how you think about something, it takes on a different meaning and produces different emotions.

I knew I couldn't let anything penetrate my armor of positivity. I didn't know what type of a battle I'd be facing, but I knew it needed to be fought with a relentless faith that everything would eventually be fine. That armor encapsulated every thought of every waking moment. *Act as if* I would be healthy soon. *Feed the positive thought bubbles.*

I could have thought, "I *have* to go to the hospital to get chemotherapy." But I chose to think, "I *get* to go to my chemo spa." Either way, I was still going to the same place for the same amount of time and would experience the same insertion of the needle. Once I reframed the process with a positive spin I no longer dreaded it.

In fact, I used my chemo spa days to tackle aspirations I hadn't previously carved out time for. If sitting in a chair with a needle penetrating my skin and shooting poison into my body isn't a wake-up call that we all have an expiration date, I don't know what is. I chose to use the five uninterrupted hours of each treatment to work on my bucket list. Every three weeks for one year I walked in, got hooked up, pulled out my laptop, and started working.

One of my top goals was to remake the *Nutcracker* with a modern, urban twist. I had danced in the *Nutcracker* for 15 years, and it had been a goal of mine for well over two decades to produce an urban version of the classic ballet in order to bring a new audience to Tchaikovsky's tale with its iconic music. So I wrote. Within four months I had completed a draft and been introduced to an agent who brought the project to Warner Bros. They bought it!

NBC optioned my version of the *Nutcracker* for a two-hour Movie of the Week, but unfortunately, as of this writing, the project has been shelved. The point is, I wasn't sitting in a chair getting poisoned in an effort to stay alive, I was using that alone time to live my life to the fullest.

A few months into my chemo I was riding up the elevator with another woman and saw she had pushed the button for the sixth floor, the chemo spa floor. So I cheerfully asked, "Are you heading to the chemo floor?" She replied, "Yes, I *have* to get chemotherapy." And I cheerfully said, "No, we *get* to get chemotherapy. We *get* to receive something that will hopefully make us better." Her expression showed me that she was not interested in hearing anything positive or cheerful about the chemotherapy experience.

It turns out, though, that my positive attitude isn't just a tool to annoy people in elevators. A peer-reviewed article appearing in the *Canadian Medical Association Journal* looked at 16 different studies spanning 30 years for a variety of ailments and the research absolutely confirmed that patients who expressed positive expectations had better health outcomes and faster recovery times.

So, regardless of how I was feeling, whenever I was asked, "How are you doing?" I always replied, "Great! Life is amazing!" And, I told my fellow coaches, the team, and Bobby regardless if I was not feeling great to not to treat me like I was sick.

Our athletes and friends thought I was trying to put a positive spin on a not-so-great situation, but I really believed it. I remember when Ariana Berlin, one of our alumna asked me, "Miss Val, how can you say you're great when you have cancer in your breast?" I replied, "I have a small malignant tumor in my breast that is getting hit with some very powerful stuff. The rest of me feels great, I have a ton of energy, and I'm having a blast living life. Why would I let a little ball in my boob ruin any part of my day? And don't you dare treat me like I'm sick! I'm not sick. Sick is when you feel like crap and have the flu. I feel *great*, therefore I'm not sick."

Just as cancer can spread if not treated properly, I didn't want the negativity to spread either. I didn't want to magnify this part of my life but rather enhance the positivity around me. I didn't and don't have time to waste on the negative. To be honest, though, I remember hitting the refresh button a lot during those months.

The year following my diagnosis was the best one of my life. Yes, you heard me right. I say that without reservation and having a deep understanding of what the diagnosis meant.

One Thursday during that year Ellette Craddock, one of our athletes, asked if we could meet later in my office. I was getting ready to leave our team training for a chemo spa appointment and I told her, "My chemo spa is sure screwing up my day." To which she replied, "Yes, but Miss Val it's giving you a lot more days."

Ahh, perspective. My message was getting through.

Chapter Nineteen

Choosing to Thrive

"My mission is not merely to survive, but to thrive, and to do so with some passion, some compassion, some humor, and some style."

—MAYA ANGELOU

I feel grateful to have expressed enough curiosity about the discomfort in my breast to have it checked out. My mother got cancer in the early 1980s at a time when it wasn't talked about; there was a weird vibe around it. Things were different then. My mother dealt with pain and blood in her stools for six months before she sought medical attention, and by the time she met with her doctors it was too late. It pains me to say this, but my mother's doctor told me she could have been treated had she gotten checked sooner. My mother was 53 when she died. I was 54 when I first felt the lump. Being reminded what my mom went through got me to see my doctor as soon as possible. I'm here today because I did.

As a leader of young women, I saw that my unfortunate news was a rare opportunity to try to educate and empower them, and perhaps even help save their lives. Yes, feeling a hard pea in the breast is still a warning sign, but so are other symptoms including lumps, pain, or changes in breast size. Still, when I went to the doctor, the last thing I thought they were going to tell me was that I had cancer. So, I asked the athletes on the team if they wanted to feel the malignant tumor in my breast.

I recognize how potentially dangerous this was, in that the gesture could have been completely misinterpreted. One part of my brain was screaming, "Stop! Human Resources is going to run over here and fire you for sexual harassment!" When the girls were putting their fingers on the side of my sports bra to feel the tumor, one of them commented how weird it was to feel "Miss Val's breast." I quickly corrected her, "No, I didn't invite you to feel my breast. I invited you to examine what a malignant tumor feels like."

I wanted to be as open as I could with the girls to answer any questions about my cancer, but I didn't want them to see it as a death sentence or treat me differently because of it. I wasn't going to let my diagnosis define me. I was determined to choreograph how I wanted the next year to play out, which for the most part meant defining my experiences in my terms.

We all have gone through or will go through extremely difficult and challenging times in life, perhaps including being diagnosed with a serious illness, enduring the death of a loved one, being hurt in a serious accident, and so on. No one is exempt from having to deal with the hard stuff. It gets touchy, though, when we start relating our misfortunes to the misfortunes of others. Even if I'm diagnosed with the same exact type of disease as someone else, there are so many other variables that go into each of our lives that neither of us should feel comfortable saying, "Oh, I know exactly how you feel."

My conscious self took control over how I chose to handle my cancer diagnosis. I've never told my father, because at the time he was 92 years old and I knew he would worry too much, so if you cross paths with him, please don't tell him, it will just make him worry. (If you're concerned he will read this, he won't. While he's still painting up a storm at 96, his eyesight doesn't allow him to read much.)

When I chose to tell our team and coaching staff, I asked them to keep it on the down low. Since I had gotten randomly chosen for the second group in the chemo study I knew I wouldn't lose my hair, so there would be no visible signs that I had cancer. It wasn't a secret, I just wanted to make everything about that year of chemo and surgeries as normal as possible for me and everyone else; I didn't want the gymnastics world to address it every time we went to a competition.

I actually chose to share my cancer saga with the world the following year at the end of our Breast Cancer Awareness meet.

I know this is not really important in the broader scheme of things, but just allow me to say that I'm not a fan of how pink is used in promoting breast cancer awareness. I think it's wonderful that almost every male and female sport has chosen to don pink attire for their competitions each October in support of Breast Cancer Awareness month. However, when you add up all the pink paraphernalia out there on just the football teams alone, I can't escape thinking about how much of that money for awareness could have instead gone into research. If I'm asked, I'll say that a simple pink sticker on a helmet or a pink ribbon on a jersey is enough to show support and start the conversation.

I got lucky, and I know it. My cancer was detected early, at stage 1. According to the American Cancer Society, the five-year survivorship rate for stage 1 and stage 2 breast cancer is 72–99 percent. Stage 4, advanced stage breast cancer, also known as metastatic breast cancer (MBC), has a five-year survivorship rate of 22 percent. MBC is defined as cancer that originated in the breast and has metastasized or spread outside the breast to another part or organ of the body.

Three years after my worldview changed that spring day in 2014 with a phone call I took on the side of the road, I found myself in a conversation with Dikla Benzeevi. Dikla is a volunteer patient advocate and navigator for the MBC community. Without thinking about what I was saying, I was telling Dikla how lucky I was because not only had my cancer been caught at stage 1, but it also had been caught at a time when this kind of cancer was treatable. As I've already said, had I received my diagnosis 10 years earlier it might have been a death sentence. As soon as I said this, my heart stopped. I knew that Dikla had the same type of breast cancer as I did, but she was diagnosed 15 years before I was. By the time the additional therapies for HER2-positive cancer had been created, her cancer had already spread.

When Dikla and I first spoke she had just gotten out of a four-day stay in the hospital to treat a very painful, partial small bowel obstruction that was due to extreme intestinal inflammation caused by some of her clinical trial cancer medications. Since 2002, Dikla has been on 16 different cancer medications in different doses and combinations. You would never know from seeing Dikla that she has been dealing with MBC for 15 years. This is something else I've learned: for Dikla and many others with MBC, the physical and medical struggles and challenges are usually not visible. The stereotypical look of someone who has cancer is not necessarily a bald head and feeble body.

I was beyond amazed to hear Dikla say how grateful she was that she hadn't needed surgery for her bowel obstruction and that the cause of the inflammation wasn't from a tumor. She went on to enumerate her blessings that she was already feeling better. Dikla smiled and told me how nice it was to have an appetite again as she slowly ate her small bowl of soup.

I will admit that I have some survivor's guilt (appropriate use of the word "survivor" here, I think, but a word I'm typically not a fan of). Especially after meeting someone like Dikla, where the only difference between us is the advanced science that was available to me—and even then I got lucky with the specialized treatment I received.

My general dislike for the word "survivor" is that throughout humanity millions of people have died from any number of things, and we don't bestow such a heroic designation on those who didn't die. People die from the flu. People die from car accidents. People die from going to the dentist. Since you haven't died from any of those things you are a survivor. See how awkward that feels? That's how I feel about the term "survivor" as it relates to cancer.

This reminds me of a conversation I recently had with Jordyn Wieber. She was one of the brave young women who came forward about the sexual abuse she suffered from Larry Nassar. She told me she did not like being referred to either as a victim nor a survivor. In fact, here's what she said in a speech she gave:

The next step for me was shifting my perspective of what it means to be a victim. I hated that word. I heard people telling me, "You are not a victim you are a survivor." The word survivor still didn't resonate with me. I didn't want to add another word to my identity because of the sexual abuse I had endured. I asked myself, why do I need a label to remind me or tell me how I am supposed to feel or live? This experience does not define me. The things that have happened to you in life DO NOT define you. Yes, I was a victim, the key word in that statement is "was." I was a victim when he abused me, but I am no longer a victim. I decided to free myself from that label.

This is so powerful. Jordyn has chosen to dictate how she wants others to perceive her; she is taking total control of her life. That is the *opposite* of being a victim. I love her comment about not wanting to add another word to her identity because of something she didn't choose.

Instead of survive, I prefer the word "thrive!" To thrive means to grow, develop, and prosper, and is exactly how I would describe the way I chose to live my life from the moment I found out I had cancer. Since that time, I have embraced more of what life has to offer than even I thought was possible.

While I was going through chemotherapy I had a very understandable excuse to take the year off. Instead, I chose to live my life as "normally" as possible. I respected the severity of the situation and addressed my physical, mental, and emotional health with extra care, but I was also determined to live this chapter of my life with renewed zest. During that gymnastics season I missed only one meet, against Florida, because of the chemo.

I made many other meaningful choices during those 12 months. The first thing I decided to do was consistently work out. This was actually one of my doctor's first recommendations. It had been 34 years since I'd stopped dancing, and I still hadn't found any type of workout that interested me enough to keep it up consistently and with a sense of commitment.

Living in Los Angeles I figured I should learn to love running, weight lifting, boot camp, or roller blading, all of which the rest of the city seemed to adore. Well, I am a horrible runner and have never, ever enjoyed it. Weight lifting and boot camp felt torturous and roller blading was just not my thing; I spent more time getting up from the ground than gliding along.

I didn't realize it at the time, but the biggest problem was that none of those exercises included an artistic release for me. Then I decided to try something new: Pilates. The moment I started the first exercise I felt at home. Traditional Pilates is a ballet barre (or the first half of a ballet class), only lying on your back. This is a discipline that my muscles understood. Another reason I embraced Pilates is because I don't sweat in the class. So I can wake up, put on my makeup, do my hair, go to an early morning Pilates class, and then go straight to work without having to touch up anything. Yes!

Before my cancer diagnosis I bought into the idea that the harder and longer I worked at my job the more successful I would be. The problem was I had sidelined many of the passions that fueled me in physical, mental, and emotionally creative ways. One of the amazing gifts I have been given working at UCLA is their understanding of my need to be creative. Not winning a championship and then going to San Diego to choreograph acrobats is not something a lot of schools would approve of. One year I asked Dr. Holland, our associate athletic director, if she had a problem with my extracurriculars and she said that on the contrary, she knew that it was through my other creative outlets that I refueled my passion for my work with the team. She felt I was actually a better coach because of all of my creative pursuits outside of UCLA. It took my cancer diagnosis before I decided to unabashedly pursue them, and they include writing this book!

Dark times do not have to define you; they can actually lead you to a more fulfilled life.

Sometimes it feels like life is checking to see if I'm paying attention. Years ago I started noticing that when I looked at a digital clock I would see identical numbers displayed—like when I woke in the middle of the night I noticed the clock read 2:22. This past year, on most mornings, I wake up at 5:55 a.m. even though my alarm is set for 6:15 a.m. Over and over again I've had this awakening where I see identical numbers being displayed.

I looked this phenomenon up and discovered it's something called "number synchronicity." In laymen's terms it basically means that you are in sync with the universe and at the exact place in life you're supposed to be. I choose to look at it like God is winking at me, telling me I'm on track for what I'm supposed to be doing in life.

Gymnastics is all a numbers game. Every toe point and wobble are given a number. This past gymnastics season number synchronicity was too blatant to ignore inside and outside the gym. One example, in midseason when the team returned from their holiday break, we all went to see the movie *The Greatest Showman*. Shortly after the movie started there was a glitch and the movie stopped playing, only to resume a few minutes later. When the picture hit the screen again one of our athletes said to me, "Miss Val, you're going to want to know this, it's 4:44."

I continued to notice number synchronicity throughout the next four months leading up to our national championship. In the last week God must have totally been messing with me because it happened *all* the time. Two days before we left for the championship, I was having a facial and told the esthetician the story of when I heard God say, "Be anxious for nothing and grateful for all things," after I was informed I had breast cancer. My esthetician said she got chills, and at that moment everything in the room flicked off and on. She was mildly freaked out because it wasn't like a plug came loose from the wall. Nope, everything shut down, then came back on: the lights, the music, and paraffin warming machine…I asked her what time it was. She said, "2:22." After the facial, as she was waiting for me to gather my things, she asked the esthetician in the room next to us if the lights had flickered during her facial. They had not.

Number synchronicity happened again the night before the national championship during our Blue versus Gold team challenge. As I've mentioned, I don't do a pregame speech and instead we do team challenges the night before each of our road competitions— at the end of each challenge the scores for each team are something like 256 to 278. In all of the many years we've been doing this, the teams' scores have *never* been tied. That night the team totals were 333 to 333!

Now, I want to make clear I don't believe God cares about sports. I simply can't imagine with all the needs in the world he would spend any amount of time blessing one team, program, coach, or athlete with a divine gift to excel above all others. I do believe, however, that I was possibly being reminded to stay the course and to maintain my balance. I like to think he was giving me an "atta girl."

The final day of the 2018 NCAA championship, the Super Six,

I decided to not get on my phone and check social media. My intention was to keep my energy focused internally, on our team, and not externally. When I got up from lunch, out of habit I checked my phone and hit the Twitter app. What popped up on my screen took my breath away. There was a photograph of the page from Philippians 4 out of the Bible with the part underlined that I had heard from God: "Be anxious for nothing..." and paraphrased "Be grateful for all things." I smiled, put my phone away, and made the conscious choice to enjoy this last time this team would be competing together.

Before leaving for the arena, I was in my hotel room and looking out the window having a chat with God and promising to not get anxious and to continue to hit the refresh button of gratitude and joy. I knew we had a championship-caliber team with a legitimate shot at coming out on top but that it would require every one of our athletes to reach the top of Coach Wooden's Pyramid of Success—Competitive Greatness. And even then the numbers would have to line up. In truth we were facing stiff competition with the No. 1-ranked Oklahoma Sooners looking to win their fourth championship in five years. As I was having my chat with God, I kid you not... a rainbow appeared.

We began the Super Six competition on the floor exercise event. It's a great event for us, but we would have preferred to finish our competition on floor since we were ranked No. 1 in the country and we view the floor as a party and we like to end competitions with a party. We brought good energy and did well, but not great. On that day we finished fourth as a team on the floor.

The next event was vault. At the end of the regular season we were ranked fourth in the country on vault and uneven bars. Again, we did well but not great. We finished the competition in fifth place on the event. After the first two rotations we had a bye and headed to the locker room in fourth place overall.

Chris Waller, one of the fiercest competitors I've ever coached with, decided to stay in the arena for the first part of the bye rotation. As he describes it, he watched one routine of each team and realized that no one was having a lights-out type of meet. It was then he had his *Rain Man* moment and started calculating that if we "PR'd" (hit our personal records) on the last two events, bars and beam, we could possibly win the meet. He roared back into the locker room and gave a passionate, blaring, *Rocky*-esque speech that went something like this:

WE'RE CHAMPIONS! WE DON'T QUIT UNDER ANY CIRCUMSTANCE. WE'RE GOING TO FIGHT OR CELEBRATE OR PARTY OR WORK OR WHATEVER IT IS YOU DO, WE'RE GOING TO GO TO THE END... EVERY MOMENT, EVERY SECOND FOR THE REST OF THIS DAY. WE'VE BEEN BUSTING ASS AS CHAMPIONS ALL YEAR AND WE'RE GOING TO FINISH THIS THING LIKE CHAMPIONS. ALL RIGHT, LET'S GO!

I didn't know it at the time, but I would learn later that after our first two events our chance of winning was less than 3 percent. ESPN must have known this because they didn't even bother broadcasting the start of our uneven bar rotation. In general, unless there is a reason that I absolutely need to know scores, I prefer to not know where we stand. For the most part, the routines are set. There is no offense or defense in gymnastics. Every once in a while I will need to make strategic choices to switch a skill or two in a routine, but those times are very rare. It's simply a matter of everyone performing their best when their best is needed. We were heading to the uneven bar rotation and there weren't any options for switching skills so I didn't need to know scores.

The competition was tight and the teams ahead of us weren't counting any mistakes. We needed excellence and that's what we achieved. Nia Dennis and Anna Glenn started us off with phenomenal routines; in fact, Anna earned a personal best score. Returning from shoulder surgery, Madison Kocian had only competed bars in the one competition before the championship. She hit a remarkable routine that wound up being the fifth best score of the entire meet. Senior Janay Honest, who walked on the team her freshman year, closed out her career by receiving a perfect 10 from one of the four judges—the only 10 she received in her entire UCLA career. Fifth in our rotation was Christine "Peng-Peng" Lee. She came over to me and asked for a hug. Knowing this was the second-to-last routine she would ever compete, I couldn't hold my emotions in and began to well up. I didn't feel that now was the time to get sappy and I told her, "Not now Peng." She didn't ask but commanded, "I NEED A HUG." Later she would tell me she needed that hug to calm down and get her energy in check. I'm so glad I complied. I walked away wiping my tears while Peng stunned the arena with a perfect 10—her default (and yes, the description of her default in this book was written months before this championship). Last up was Kyla Ross, who held her handstands so long you could have taken a coffee break under the bars before she swung around. By the time the rotation concluded our uneven bar squad earned the second highest bar score in NCAA championship history. And with that we headed to balance beam...still in fourth place.

At this point I honestly thought we were playing for third...second at best. I didn't know it at the time, but our balance beam lineup would need to average a 9.95. To put this in further perspective, not a single competitor for the entire competition had scored a 9.95 and that needed to be our average.

The focus and joy our team was displaying were becoming overwhelming. Tears were already flowing from me and our athletes and we still had one rotation to go. I quickly tried to gather myself for an interview with ESPN right before our last rotation. I said to them, "It's a good thing I have no affinity for math, because in my mind we can still win this thing." It wasn't over!

Our athletes were beyond dialed in on beam. They had a glow and confidence about them that you see in athletes when they are 100 percent in the zone. Before each athlete salutes the judge to compete, I always go up to each of them and remind them of one cue. I went up to our leadoff athlete, Grace Glenn, and was ready to tell her what I always do, "tap into your inner badass." Before I could say anything she looked at me and said, "Miss V, I got this." The look in her eye was one of absolute confidence. She killed it, earning a 9.9375. The fourth highest beam score of the entire meet. Our next athlete, Madison Kocian, a 2016 Olympic gold medalist, had that same confidence and was executing a gorgeous routine, but fell on her flipping series. The rules of competition allow all teams to drop the lowest score on each event, which meant the next four athletes had to be near perfect.

Brielle Nguyen was next. Brielle had never competed at an NCAA championship before and she was now in the toughest spot of the meet...following a fall...from an Olympian. She nailed it, earning a 9.875.

Up next was Katelyn Ohashi, who two seasons prior announced to me and the rest of the team that she didn't want to be great anymore. As I started to remind her of her cue she grabbed my hand, looked me in the eye, smiled, and said, "Miss Val, this is where we thrive." She did...earning a 9.95.

Up next, Kyla Ross, a 2012 Olympic gold medalist who had actually had our only other fall of the meet, on floor during our first rotation. As I was getting ready to tell her what I always tell her before she mounts the balance beam, "Don't try to be perfect, just enjoy it," she looked me square in the eyes and with a smile on her face said, "Miss Val, I got this." Boom...9.9875.

The last competitor for us was sixth-year senior Peng, who was coming off a perfect routine on bars and would (unbeknownst to us) need a near-perfect 9.975 routine for us to win. Let me take you into the arena at this moment. Everyone in the arena, everyone watching at home on their televisions, and everyone except a handful of math whizzes felt we were playing for second at this point. This was evident by the fact that the ESPN TV cameras were camped out at the opposite end of the arena ready to capture Oklahoma's jubilation knowing they'd won their third championship in a row. LSU and Florida had completed their rotations on vault and floor, respectfully, and already knew they hadn't beat Oklahoma (as had the other two teams who completed their competition one rotation earlier, Utah and Nebraska). *Everyone*...including me and our team members...thought Oklahoma had won the meet.

I went up to Peng and was ready to tell her what I always did, "Slow down your dance." This kept her rhythm in check instead of getting too hyped up. Before I could say anything she smiled at me and said, "Miss Val, this is my last routine ever. I'm going to enjoy every moment of it." What happened next was magical. Every skill, every dance move, every smile, every movement was intentional, including looking around the arena during her dance to take in her last competitive performance. When she dismounted, the arena erupted with fans from different schools chanting "10, 10, 10, 10." Our team was sobbing because we had finished the meet with the most stellar performance we could ever imagine. Without a score we knew we had reached the top of Coach Wooden's Pyramid of Success. And then the score came up...a perfect 10. Another swell of fresh emotion and then one by one the team started pointing to the scoreboard—in seemingly slow motion the team names and final totals changed as UCLA moved to the top of the leaderboard. WHAT?!?!?!?!? With a 49.75, we had just posted the highest beam score in NCAA championship history!

Chris Waller ran up to me and hugged me and screamed, "WE JUST WON THE MEET!" I turned to my left and the camera operators were running across the arena to us in what appeared to me to be Hollywood slow motion. I had won enough championships to know that at that moment the camera operators are only interested in capturing the winning team. I started shaking my hands back and forth and saying, "No, no, no, no. Don't get too excited. This is like the Academy Awards when they opened the wrong envelope and announced the wrong movie winning. They're going to tell us any minute that they added wrong." And then I saw our athletic director, Dan Guerrero, and my husband, Bobby Field, walking across the arena to us. Wait...does this mean we really WON? WE WON THE NATIONAL CHAMPIONSHIP! HOW??? Even the slightest wobble or bent leg from any of our athletes would have kept us off the top of the podium. Instead we won by the smallest margin of victory in championship history!

I honestly believe that had I known we could win if we averaged a 9.95, I probably would have over coached. Instead of trusting each of our athletes when they told me, "Miss Val, I got this" and smiling and walking away, I probably would have said, "That's great..." and proceeded to remind them of their cues...just in case. I'm so glad I didn't. Their performances were what every athlete dreams of...free, in the zone, calm, confident, enthusiastic, and absolutely brilliant.

Since the 2018 championship I have heard a lot of people comment on how great it was to see a team win with such joy and love for each other—a potential answer to the dominating headlines of abusiveness our sport has recently endured. It saddens me that so much negativity has clouded our sport because the truth is there are many amazing coaches in the United States, teaching our youth not only great gymnastics skills but important life skills as well. Sadly they don't make the news. If I were to say what was the key ingredient that propelled us to win the 2018 Championship it would be love. Love for the sport, Love for the process, and Love for each other.

Coach Wooden used to express his regret for not having included love as one of the bricks in his Pyramid of Success. I would always argue with him that the love was intrinsically there, that the pyramid couldn't be completed without love being the mortar or binding ingredient for all the bricks.

The incredibly impressive part of this win is that our team's overwhelming emotion was pouring out even before we finished the meet and long before we had realized that we had won. The magic happened because we chose to appreciate the moment and recognize that this was the last time this team was going to be competing together. We were all living in the moment full of gratitude and love, freeing us to perform as *champions*.

Success!

Acknowledgments

I can never express enough gratitude for the man who is my husband Bobby Field. Everyone who meets him feels the same saintly energy exude from him of all that is good in life. Thank you for not just loving me but supporting me in everything I do, including writing this book. Your unwavering support, your sense of humor and your ability to flip the switch to Coach Field when I need you most is something that keeps our love fresh, fun, and vibrant.

I have assembled an amazing coaching tandem that has stayed together longer than any previous group of coaches I've had. Randy Lane actually worked with us as a coach and as a performer in the shows I choreograph at SeaWorld. He has been a part of our coaching staff for three different stints, during which time he also got his masters in acupuncture. Chris Waller was a UCLA gymnast whom I've known since he was 18 years old. After he graduated he applied for an assistant coaching position with us—twice. Both times I said, "Chris you need to grow up a bit more and go coach girls." (Chris had only coached boys at that point.) In 2002 I had a coaching vacancy and felt he was ripe for the job. I called him and said, "Hi, Chris, it's Valorie." Before I could say anything else he said, "Does this call mean I've grown up?"

Chris, Randy, and I are at times the proverbial "oil and water," but that's what I respect most about our working relationship. We can vehemently disagree with each other, and yet, through growing together as mature coaches, we've learned to shut up and listen, stay true to our beliefs, and always walk out of the room as a unified coaching staff.

Our third coach has fit in seamlessly. Olympic champion Jordyn Wieber joined our program as a team manager after earning a gold medal in the 2012 Olympic Games. Since she had "gone pro" she had been unable to compete for our team, a sadness that will stay heavy on my heart until the day I die—seriously. Jordyn lived through the challenging life of an elite gymnast and brings a wonderfully sound perspective to how to train like a champion while honoring the *person* who is the *athlete*.

My deepest gratitude to all of the coaches, athletes, and fans whom I've worked with over the years. Your dedication and love for gymnastics has inspired me to make each day a masterpiece, resulting in an unpredictable life full of joy and adventure. For all I have shared, each lesson and experience was enriched by others. I wish I could list each and every one of you, but the decades of personal relationships would require a bulging second volume for appropriate thanks.

Two people that have been with me through all of the thick and thin are literally Godsends, and what I feel are my guardian angels. One is our athletic trainer, Lorita Granger. She is the yin to my yang. I joke that she is the real leader of the UCLA gymnastics team, and in many ways it's true. She embraces her work, every student-athlete, and our staff with pure love and commitment to helping all of us be better versions of ourselves.

The other person who I have been beyond blessed to have in my life is my manager Gary Minzer. Everyone who is pursuing a dream would be lucky to have an advocate who believes in them and their mission as Gary believes in me and mine. I can't tell you how many times my most successful friends have expressed to me how much they need a Gary in their life. Thank you Gary for enthusiastically embracing all my ideas and helping to make them a reality.

A big thank-you to my co author, Coop. Writing a book has been a daunting, exhilarating, and at many times frustrating endeavor. Your patience with me while maintaining an unwavering commitment to the integrity of the stories and words written in this book is something I've recognized throughout this whole process. You are a consummate professional and a brilliant researcher and writer. I'm so glad you made the Ask to help me write this book.

I'd also like to make a very special acknowledgment and thank you to my publisher Hachette Book Group/Center Street and to my Editorial Director Kate Hartson and Associate Editor Jaime Coyne who believed in me, my life's philosophies and story and who have given me the opportunity and medium to express myself and convey my message to the world!

A noteable thank you to Kathy Lubbers, my literary agent, whose unconditional support and guidance has been so very much appreciated as we worked through all the components and process of writing this book.

And lastly, every challenging venture needs an initial spark. The spark for me to decide to write this book came from my amazing friend, Abbe Shapiro. She was one of many people who told me I needed to write a book. When I told her, "What do I have to say that hasn't already been written?" She replied, "It's not what you say but how you say it. Anything of Truth has been passed down from the dawn of man. Every generation needs new story tellers to discuss those Truths in ways we can best understand and employ." At that moment, I knew I would write this book.

About the Authors

VALORIE KONDOS FIELD is the head coach of the UCLA women's gymnastics team. She has led her team to seven NCAA championship titles and 29 Pac-12 and NCAA Regional titles. This preeminent coach was recently named the Pac-12 Coach of the Century, and in 2010, she became one of only two active coaches to be inducted into the UCLA Athletic Hall of Fame.

This is the first book for STEVE COOPER, a journalist who started his career at *Entrepreneur* nearly 20 years ago and has since worked with *Bloomberg, Forbes,* the *Huffington Post, BusinessWeek, TheStreet,* and many others. Cooper is also the cofounder and editor of HitchedMag.com. He resides in Southern California with his wife, Jessica O'Beirne, who hosts GymCastic, the world's No. 1 gymnastics podcast.